WISDOM ON THE CAMINO

WISDOM  ON THE CAMINO

A SPIRITUAL JOURNEY
SHARING FORGIVENESS AND POSSIBILITIES
TO INSPIRE THE REST OF YOUR LIFE

KATHLEEN DONNELLY ISRAEL

ISBN: 978-1-7369998-0-6

This book is dedicated to…

My late husband Ron
and to our grown children, Lisa, Peter, Carla, Cecilia
and John, who have kept me grounded
all these years.

View the portfolio of my pictures
As my gift to you.

Read this first

People who have read Wisdom on the Camino have expressed their desire to see the photos of my journey. It would have been cost prohibitive to include them in the book.

To say thank you for buying my book, I would like to give you the experience of following along with me by viewing the pictures from my pilgrimage as you read chapter by chapter.

To opt-in to view the pictures go to:
http://wisdomonthecamino.com/pictures
be sure to bookmark the link so you can join me as you read.

TABLE OF CONTENTS

PREFACE

This book has been a joy for me to write. Remembering my time on the Camino Santiago has been medicine for my soul. The Camino Santiago de Compostela is a holy pilgrimage. I am a Roman Catholic, and I love my faith. I have, in the past, described myself as an ethnic Catholic. My faith is such a part of who I am, it's actually my ethnicity as much as or more so than my ancestral heritage. I have been studying spirituality my whole life. The beauty of the mysticism on this pilgrimage wasn't lost on me. Through the years and through my studies, I have developed some philosophies and wisdom that I shared with my fellow pilgrims on the Camino. I have included the stories of what I shared with them in these pages. I've changed some names because I shared personal stories and didn't want to identify anyone. I may have remembered some of the facts incorrectly. I didn't write everything down. I hope you'll enjoy my story of love and beauty. If you don't share my faith, I invite you to enjoy my story as an ethnic study and not be offended by my faith. I believe that God is bigger than religion. I also believe if you're talking about God but you're not talking about Love, then you're not really talking about God.

I decided to travel the Camino years before I could go. My friend, Judy, from grade school went on the Camino. I was inspired. Even though she got blisters and walked with bloody feet, I could tell that she was fulfilling a wonderful dream for herself. My dreams of what my husband Ron and I would do in our retirement were shattered when he got Parkinson's disease. I thought we would be riding our bicycles across France in our retirement. That wasn't to be. I found another dream to look forward to: making a pilgrimage on the Camino Santiago de Compostela. I knew I wanted to do the whole thing from France all the way across Spain. I knew I would have to wait till Ron was done with his disease. He died in August 2018.

In a spiritual reading after his death that my friend, Josemar, recorded for me, I was told, "Kathleen, you have had this urge to explore the old country, to reach for that feeling, to reach for that soil, to reach for that connection that goes back farther than you've thought so far, that goes back so deep and it goes back in the blood, really far, and this is a really strong deep earthy kind of feeling and this energy is moving through you right now…"

January 2019, I started to prepare for my trip. I read books, watched videos, and went to lectures. I learned how to pack lightly and started gathering my essentials. I bought and returned four backpacks before I found the right one. The same with clothing. I searched the web for lightweight and sun-protection clothing. I bought items, tried them on and returned them if they didn't fit or if they weren't as light weight as I needed. I got Gore-Tex waterproof boots because I knew it would be rainy. I got them an extra size and a half larger because feet swell. My sleeping bag was a youth size so it would weigh less. I wore as much negative ion (-ion) clothing as I could because they wick moisture away from the body and the -ions impart comfort. I made a sleep sack nighty out of two -ion stoles so I would be covered with -ions at night. I wore -ion underwear and socks. I brought -ion buffs (small tubular scarfs) and a -ion beanie. I believe the reason I didn't get any blisters was because of the negative ion socks I wore every day.

I renewed my passport and got my airfare. I set up bed and breakfasts for my time in Paris ahead of my adventure. I got a new smart phone so I would have good battery life, and it could be my camera. It also served as my computer for making reservations and for finding my way on the Camino.

After arriving in Paris March 28, 2019, I spent six days there to make sure I didn't have jet lag when starting my pilgrimage. I got to St. Jean Pied de Port, the official starting point for the Camino Frances, on April 4 and spent the next 66 days on the Camino, including delays for sickness and staying two nights at a hotel every weekend. I took Holy Week off as well. I spent my 70th birthday on the Camino.

This book highlights many of my experiences along the Camino. From St. Jean Pied de Port in France through beautiful country side, weather, friendships, religious experiences, and illnesses to the completion of my Camino in Santiago in Spain. It is truly a story of the good the bad and the beautiful.

One of the reasons I wasn't afraid to travel the Camino alone was because I wasn't really alone. My guardian angels were with me. I have four whom I know personally. They protect me at home and they went with me to Spain.

People ask me what I got out of the Camino. I learned how to take care of myself, get my needs met, and stand up for myself. My time on the Camino was sacred time. I learned that my whole life going forward is sacred time. All of life is a Camino and every moment is sacred.

INTRODUCTION

The Camino Santiago de Compostela or The Camino Frances, is a 500-mile pilgrimage across northern Spain. It has been in existence since the 1200s. There are many stories about its beginning. One story tells that St. James, one of the 12 apostles of Jesus, came to Spain as a missionary but he made few converts. When he returned to Jerusalem, he was martyred and his body was taken back to Spain on a boat and by angels. He was buried in Spain. His grave was found and after St. James appeared and helped the Christians have victory over the Muslims in Spain, the pilgrimage started. When they tried to resurrect the pilgrimage in modern times the trail, which had been an old Roman road, was pretty much intact except where freeways had been built over parts of it.

Many trails lead to Santiago. A more northern route along the northern coast of Spain is called the Camino del Norte and a rough country one is the Camino Primitivo. The routes through Portugal are called the Camino Portugues, another starts in Madrid, and many more. They all end up at the Santiago de Compostela Cathedral in Santiago, Spain.

There are as many reasons to walk the Camino as there are pilgrims. Some want a spiritual experience, some want a physical accomplishment, some are looking for a change in their life or to get unstuck from depression. Some go because they heard about it and their soul wanted to go.

The albergues are like hostels along the Camino. They're run by organizations, individuals, families, or municipalities. A large organization oversees the albergues and ensures they keep a standard for a healthy environment. The price to stay in the albergues is very inexpensive for a bunk. Some serve dinner, especially if there are no restaurants in town, and some have a kitchen where pilgrims can cook their own meals, especially if there's a market in town. Many towns have supermercados or supermarkets; others have little shops where pilgrims can buy a few foods to cook or eat on the road. A bar is a place to get coffee or beer and a snack and to use the restroom. Most towns have a bar. You can find hotels along the Camino also. They usually have pilgrim rates, but they're more expensive than the albergues. Some albergues have private rooms for pilgrims but at a higher cost for the lodging.

The scallop shell and the yellow arrow are important motifs on the Camino. Statues and pictures of St. James show him with a shell over his breast or on his bag. The towns along the Camino display the shell in celebration of the Camino. Sidewalks, fences, and buildings are adorned with the shell. Pilgrims wear a shell on their pack identifying themselves. The shell could signify an opened hand, a symbol of the good works expected of the pilgrims or it could signify all of the many roads that lead to Santiago. The yellow arrows are displayed along the Camino to help the pilgrims find and stay on the Camino trail. The yellow arrows are sometimes painted on streets, walls, and fences. Sometimes, the yellow arrows are on official ceramic tiles set into cement markers showing the kilometer reading at that spot. All along the Camino many creative displays of the shell and the yellow arrow show the way and gladden the hearts of grateful pilgrims.

The Pilgrim's Credential is a folded thick sheet of paper on which a stamp and date are recorded at each place the pilgrim stays along the way. The presented credential lets the albergues know they're admitting a true pilgrim. Each pilgrim must present their passport and their credential to be admitted to the albergue. The passport information is recorded in an official book. It lets the government know where the pilgrims are daily. The Compostela or certificate of completion, is given to those pilgrims who walk at least the last 100 kilometers of the Camino Santiago.

Pilgrims are expected to keep going along the Camino. Albergues are housing for just one night. Pilgrims are expected to be up and gone early in the morning usually by 8 am. If a pilgrim wants to stay longer, they must get a hotel room. The same is true for the special pilgrim dinners. The restaurants that provide the inexpensive pilgrim dinners don't want to have you come back the next night. These inexpensive amenities are given happily and generously to pilgrims who, by definition, keep going.

The best times to make a Camino Santiago de Compostela pilgrimage are in the spring and fall when the weather is mild. The summer brings the heat and crowds who all vie for limited bunk space and create a procession effect, eliminating solitude along the Camino. The winter is icy and dangerous. Although the religious celebrations of Holy Week and Easter on the Camino are unique and breathtaking experiences, many of the albergues are not opened until after Easter.

Traditionally, packing lightly for traveling the Camino, pilgrims carry everything on their back every day on the pilgrimage. For those who need them, services are available that will transport packs from one albergue or hotel to the next destination for a small fee. Also available are buses and taxis that will transport pilgrims who run out of time, are injured, sick, or tired; or for some reason, not able to walk. I met a young man who was taking taxis from albergue to albergue, the whole way. He didn't want to tell me his story.

Even though the cost of lodging and food for pilgrims is low, the Camino is a huge part of the economy in the villages of northern Spain. The bars know that the pilgrims will buy something to use the restroom. The albergues keep their costs low so they can provide for the pilgrims inexpensively.

In ancient times, the Knights Templars were protectors of pilgrims on the Camino Santiago. It is said they still are there, protecting the Pilgrims. Every time I saw the image of the Knights Templar Santiago Order cross made out of daggers, I imagined that they were close somewhere and felt safe. I saw a lot of white horses in fields along the Camino. I imagined that their ancestors were the horses ridden by the Knights Templars. I also read that St. James was said to have ridden a white horse.

WISDOM ON THE CAMINO

CHAPTER 1

GETTING TO THE CAMINO

When the cab got me to my destination, it was almost midnight. The cab driver stopped at the top of the street and, pointing, said, "It's down there." I peered down the street, which had no lights then looked at him in disbelief. I don't usually walk alone down dark streets at night in strange towns. I grabbed my pack, paid the guy, and walked down the street. I had my hiking boots to protect me, after all, and a mini flashlight to find my way. I assumed that my guardian angels were on duty as well. A bit of the Moon was shining, so it wasn't entirely dark.

I checked the addresses on each doorway with my flashlight. My address wasn't on any of the doorways. I texted my host. She texted me back, telling me it was the white door and I should open it, go to the third floor, and turn right, and it was the first door. Oh man, open a door that didn't have an address at almost midnight? Okay, so I found a white door with no address and opened it gingerly. It led to a courtyard. I found an elevator with a light inside, how nice. I went up to the third floor. Out of the elevator, I turned right and went to hopefully the correct door and knocked. The lady answered and ushered me to my room, telling me she was glad I had arrived and scolding me for being so late and not contacting her when I got in. I didn't know she wasn't accepting calls, just texts.

Earlier that day, leaving Paris, I took a jet to Biarritz. I had heard they didn't allow hiking poles in carry-on luggage. I also had an all-important Swiss Army knife which couldn't be in my carry-on. Since there was a mix up on my ticket, the airlines offered me a free checked sports equipment. Perfect, thank you, God. I checked my pack and poles as sporting equipment.

When I got to Biarritz, it was late. As we disembarked the plane, snow was on the temporary stairway. Burr! I went inside the terminal and asked where to catch the bus. They pointed to a door. The bus stop was surrounded on three sides by glass partitions and had benches to sit on. I tried several times to call my host to tell her I was there, but there was no answer. I waited at the bus stop till my hands were numb; and still, no bus came. I had contacted the bus line a month before and told them when my plane would be in, and they said okay. Now I had waited way too long, watching as each vehicle drove by and hoping it was my bus. I went inside and spoke to a pleasant uniformed lady sitting behind a desk who said the buses ran only in the summer. I was devastated. She suggested that I take a cab. Ugh, the last cab I used took me on a wild goose chase to ring up the bill. Cabs were parked outside in a queue. I asked the first driver how much it would be for a ride into Bayonne and showed him the address. He said 30 euros. I got in and prayed. He got me where I wanted to go, sort of.

Being in my warm and comfortable B&B made me forget my trouble getting there. My room was great.

It had a big comfy curvy iron bed with a blue cotton duvet cover over a lofty down comforter. I noticed the heater didn't seem to work. A shelving unit had fun amenities: a hot pot, bottled water, cocoa, tea, cookies, and brochures about the area. I cleaned up in the very modern bathroom down the hall, had a cup of bouillon that I brought from Paris, and went to bed.

The next morning, I had to be out at 7:30 to catch my train. I met my host in the kitchen. She apologized that her boyfriend didn't turn on the power to the heater and scolded me some more for being late. I found out that she was a psychotherapist. I thought it was odd that a therapist was trying to make me feel bad for being late, as if I could have controlled the situation. She walked out with me to the top of the street, where the cab driver left me, she pointed in the direction of the train station. I hoped she was pointing to the large building with raw wooden sides and a turquoise-colored roof with a cupola on top on the other side of town. She was on her way to work. I was glad to continue my adventure. I walked by a small merry-go-round and over a bridge across a river, not sure where I was going. I asked a man where the train station was, and he said that he was going there so I followed him.

In the station, I looked around for anyone who looked like they were going on the Camino. A woman and a man about my age had packs and boots on, a couple of young men had packs, and a young woman toted a pack and wore boots too. I felt better, like I was in the right place. I'm not used to taking trains. My ticket that I purchased online was saved on my phone. I asked a station attendant where the train would leave from. He told me it would be announced later. Ugh, I didn't want to hear that I couldn't put myself in the right place and just wait there. I spoke to the woman who was my age and she didn't seem concerned about not knowing where the train would leave from. I sat down, got an apple out of my pack, and ate it while I waited. When the train came into the station, it stopped in one place to unload and then went forward to pick up its passengers. Everyone else got on the train, so I asked, "St Jean Pied de Port?" to the smartly uniformed station man and he nodded. I took a deep breath and got on. I sat in front of the woman I'd spoken to earlier and asked her if she were going on the Camino. She smiled and said yes. We introduced ourselves. Her name was Diane. She was from Australia and just a year younger than me. We talked about our reasons for going on the Camino. Her brother wanted them to go together, but he died, so she was going in memory of him. It turned out we were staying in the same albergue in St. Jean.

I enjoyed the trip to St. Jean Pied de Port. The scenery was gorgeous with many colors of green. We saw scurrying sheep, cattle, charming wooden fences with x motifs, hills, rivers, manicured farms, and farmhouses with outbuildings. When we got to St. Jean Pied de Port, I was surprised that the train stop seemed plain and modern, not charming like what I had imagined. A large map of the village was displayed. I started walking toward the town. Along the way, I showed some people my book and the address of my albergue. They each pointed me in the right direction. The town got more and more charming as I went on. Stores, hotels, a bank, and restaurants were all in ancient buildings retrofitted for modern times. I was delighted to see a single flower growing out of a chink in a very old rock wall. I loved it all. I got to my albergue and it was still closed.

Across the way was the pilgrim office where I could sign in. I opened the wood-framed glass door into a bare room with a wooden school table, a plastic chair for the official, and two plastic chairs on the customer side. I got in line and weighed my pack on a galvanized farm-scale hung from the ceiling. It was 10 kilos. A man looked at me approvingly and told me that was a good weight. I noticed a bowl of seashells with strings slipped through a hole in the top with a donation sign and money slot. I selected one and put my 2 euros in the slot. When it was my turn to sit down, a German man behind me seized the opportunity to step in front of me, assuming, I suppose, that I wasn't paying attention. I said *excuse me*, and stepped forward, grabbed the back of the chair, and sat down. His friend shook his head and pulled him back. I wasn't going to start my Camino being pushed around!

I showed the lady at the desk my passport and she gave me a packet in a plastic zip bag with my Camino credential, which she stamped, some directions for getting out of the town and onto the Camino, and a list of approved albergues along the way. She told me that it was against the law to go over the mountain to Orrison at this time, because of snow. So, I would have to go around the mountain on the way to Valcarlos and follow the directions on the extra map.

I went out and walked back to find an interesting restaurant in an old building that I passed coming in. I was hungry for breakfast. I walked in and up some tight stairs to a noisy dining room. A waitress met me and sat me at a table in the middle. At the table, I found a napkin with a picture of a blackbird. I sat there looking out at the lovely patio with vines, and big floppy yellow flowers, and birds where some people were dining. When my waitress came back, I asked her if I could sit outside. She took me to the patio. It was windy, but I preferred that to the noise inside. I ordered eggs with vegetables and coffee. I looked around at the people and tried to imagine which ones were going to walk the Camino. I had heard that some comradery developed between pilgrims on the Camino and I didn't know how to make it happen. Two women came in and sat nearby. They seemed excited and chatted together. I felt lonely without a friend to talk to. A man was sitting by himself, but I was reluctant to approach him. The breakfast filled me up and I was on my way. After I paid at the counter, the waitress smiled broadly, gave me a plastic-wrapped fruity pectin bar, and told me, "This is for the Camino." As I walked to my albergue I noticed a lot of shops with food, spices, and hiking gear were opened. I realized that I could have bought my poles and knife in St. Jean.

When I got to my albergue, The Beilari, there was a line to sign in. I was told that there was no more room. I told them I had a reservation. They asked for my name and where I was from. When I told them, they said, "Okay, you're on the list." Whew, when it was my turn, I showed my passport. They said I could get my Camino credential stamped later. The guy who checked us in introduced himself as Joseph. He was a jolly fellow. I paid for my bed, dinner, breakfast, and lunch to take with me the next day. The rules were explained to us: dinner at 6, the door closed at 9:00 pm, lights out by 9:30, breakfast at 7:00, and we had to be out by 8:00 am. There was mention that we would be woken in a special way in the morning. Joseph smiled mysteriously and whispered, "It's the angels. You'll see; it's beautiful."

After our group was signed in, Joseph took us to our room up the stairs. I got a lower bunk near the door. He said there was a clothes-washing station out on the roof. I asked him if there was soap. He told me that on the Camino, all you need is a bar of soap and you can wash your clothes, hair, teeth, and body with one bar of soap. Okay, I'm frugal. I went out on the roof patio. Right in the middle was a pan in a sink, so I commenced washing my clothes with my bar of soap and rinsed them. Then Joseph came out and showed me an amazing device. It was a centrifuge. It was great; I put my clothes in it and a piece of plastic on top, pumped it with my hand, and the water spun out so the clothes would dry fast. A bowl caught the water as it came out the spout at the bottom. I also noticed some clotheslines and a few clothespins. I had some safety pins to hang up my clothes. Safety pins keep your clothes on the line in the wind better than clothespins. I was worried that my clothes wouldn't dry in time, but Joseph said the wind would dry them in no time.

I went out into town to find a bank and a place to get a pedicure. The bank was easy. At the ATM I got

300 euros and put it in my waist wallet. Not finding a pedicure place, I asked Siri (on my iPhone) where I could get a pedicure. She found a place about a half-mile away and so I let her lead me there. I walked down lovely lanes with rock-walled gardens and flowers. I found myself in front of a large white building with a locked gate in front. I pushed the button and a man in a uniform came out to see what I wanted. It turned out that Siri led me to the police station that was a spa years ago. The policeman took me into the office and he and the other officers discussed where to send me to get a pedicure. They wrote down the address and directions on a card for me and sent me off. I followed the directions to a rambling spa on a country road that was closed. While I was sadly standing there, the spa owner drove up. She said she could see me the next day. I wouldn't be there the next day so Siri led me back to the albergue. After all of the falderal, it was almost time for dinner. So, I got my dry clothes from the clothesline on the roof and took them to my bunk.

When I arrived in the dining room, almost everyone was already at the table. Joseph was giving advice and answering questions about how to survive and live lightly on the Camino. He was a great teacher and he wanted us all to do well. Coincidentally, the owner of the albergue was also named Joseph and the cook was the owner's son. They were all working to get the dinner finished and on the table by 6 pm. Owner Joseph reminded volunteer Joseph that he was there to help get dinner on, not to talk with the guests. He hopped to it and made the salad.

The owner Joseph gathered us all around and he had a mini glass of sweet dewy before-dinner wine for each of us. He explained that we were embarking on the adventure of our lives. He had us all go around and tell why we were there. He explained that we would all get out of the Camino what we were supposed to get. It wasn't important to know what we wanted to get from the Camino because he was sure what we got would be different than what we could imagine. He asked us to go around the table and give a name to our walk. I gave my walk the name, "Deeper than I know." We ate dinner together and we met each other a bit. I was pleased that Diane, from the train, was there. Owner Joseph offered to us that some of us could stay an extra night if we needed to get more rest before we started. I knew that I would be ready to leave in the morning. I already spent my rest time in Paris, and I couldn't wait to get going. Diane said she was going to stay an extra day.

I went up to bed and got everything ready for the morning. I lay in bed wishing I were asleep. I dozed and the morning arrived before I knew it. We were awakened by the sounds of thousands of angels singing wafting up the stairway to our room. After a while, volunteer Joseph was in the hall and he made sure everyone was up. I got up, dressed warmly, and went down to breakfast. The bread was big and cut thickly. They had eggs, orange juice, pears, and cheese with honey. Joseph, the owner, was putting together our lunch sandwiches of egg and bell peppers, onion, and cheese on thick bread. He wrapped them in cellophane and handed them out. I went upstairs to get my pack. As I was leaving, volunteer Joseph was showing someone how to use the hiking sticks. I had studied walking with poles with YouTube at home but I stopped to get the gist again. We practiced up and down the hall and he made sure we did it right. He asked me how heavy my pack was and what was in it.

I rattled off my list and he suggested I leave my guide book behind and a few other things that I didn't think I could live without. I took everything with me. He reminded us to take the low road because they didn't want to have to rescue anyone off the mountain. The arrows were mostly on the ground up there and were covered with snow.

CHAPTER 2

LEAVING ST. JEAN PIED DE PORT

780 KM TO GO

I practiced my cadence with my poles on the way out of town. I could see snow-capped Orrison in the distance. I stopped into an ancient little shop that sold hiking equipment. The proprietor suggested that I get double-headed ends for my poles. He said the ones I had on there wouldn't last very long. I was glad to get the new ones.

I hiked alone a long way before I started to wonder where the turnoff to Valcarlos was. It was a beautiful day. I passed gardens of plants familiar and exotic in the neighborhood, and in the farmyards later on. I kept hiking and watching for the yellow arrow signs. I hiked 4 kilometers to a sign that said Orrison. I realized that I had missed the turnoff. I saw a man in his yard and asked him where the turnoff was. He said it was down in town. He pointed across the valley and said I could cut across. I was afraid I would get lost. Ugh, I would have to go back down to where I started. That would add 8 km on to my first day of hiking. On the way down I met with other hikers without packs who were taking a day hike. I took out the map of the directions to get out of town. It had a picture of the building where you turn. I found that building and took the turnoff and walked out of town the other way. The arrows weren't as plentiful as they were on the other road. I was glad to see each one. I got to an area where I didn't know which way to go. I saw some other hikers and followed them, hoping they knew where to go. When I got outside of town, I saw a flat road and one that went up a hill. The others went up the hill, then I saw a yellow arrow and knew I was on the right track. I went past farms with sheep and cattle, their bells clanging as they ate. I climbed up a steep mountain and down the other side. Then up another and down. The freeway looped along at the bottom of the hills. I was tempted to just follow the freeway but I wasn't sure when the correct road would veer off so I continued to walk up the hills and down the other sides. I decided that the pilgrim road went across the land and the hills were in the path of the pilgrim road so I was following the ancient path of the pilgrims. I was so glad that it didn't rain as forecast.

I got into Valcarlos around 4:30. I showed my guide book to a man on the street pointing to the address of the municipal albergue. He pointed to the edge of a parking area next to a sheer drop-off. I went over to the edge and noticed a railed stairway going down along the cliff. I walked down to a locked door with a window in it. As I started to knock, a man opened the door and let me in. It was a plain kitchen-dining room painted white with grey melamine counters and an old stove and sink. A large table stood near the stove and a couple of smaller tables were closer to the door. I walked in and noticed a lady, who turned out to be Shirley from Holland, cooking. Some more people were sitting at the table by the stove with a bottle of wine. Someone told me to pick a bunk, and go to the store, and tell the lady who took care of the place that I was there. A tall young attractive woman, who turned out to be Grace, came up to me and said that she thought I would be more comfortable in one of the hotels in town. I told her that I was on a low budget and that the municipal albergue would be fine for me. I went into the bunk room and selected the only lower bunk that was left. Thank You, God. After laying out my sleeping bag and stowing my pack, I went up to the market. I noticed a young woman looking around the shelves too. We talked about the different canned and jarred protein options, chicken, sardines, tuna, and some mystery meat paste. I got some groceries for dinner and breakfast and lunch the next day. At the check-out, I told the lady behind the cash register that I wanted to stay in the albergue. She asked me if I claimed a bunk and said she would be down later to sign us all in and I could pay her then. Before I got to the exit door, I noticed that there was a bar that shared the space next to the market. Wow, I could use a glass of wine. The lady I met in the store had a glass of wine too. It was only 90 cents, less than 1 euro! The wine was red, dry, and lovely. We talked in her limited English and my limited Spanish about the weather. I couldn't figure out if she was a pilgrim or not. I gathered my stuff and walked back to the muni.

I was greeted when I entered by a small crowd of pilgrims sitting and standing around the table by the stove. There were a few bottles of wine on the table. I was offered a glass and a seat. I immediately wished I had bought a bottle to share too. A friendly guy, who turned out to be Daniel from Germany, told me that his new friend was very sad. I looked at his friend, sitting next to me, and asked why he was sad. He said he had three friends die within a short time and it made him so sad that his life had stopped. That's why he came to the Camino. I told him that I knew what he was going through. My husband died in August and my mom died in December. He looked at me with compassion and said that he was so sorry for my loss and we had something in common. He was Samir from Los Angeles. Daniel told me to guess how old Samir was. Samir said, "Yes, guess how old I am." I considered his looks and took a wild stab and said 40.

His eyes got big and he said, "That's right! How did you do that?" We shared about why we were there. I lamented that I got a speeding ticket right before I left home and I was going to have to do traffic school on the Camino. The Wi-Fi wasn't good. Samir suggested that I get another person to do it for me. Someone suggested that Wi-Fi was better in the hotels. So that was a possibility for later on.

Across the table, I was pleased to see a woman from the Beilare where I stayed in St. Jean. She was Terry from Oregon. She was sipping a glass of wine and enjoying the conversation. I smiled and waved at her and she waved back in recognition. A brother and sister, Justin and Christina, from Canada were there too. We all sat around enjoying talking and meeting each other. I discovered a lot of cookware in the cupboard to make my dinner of zucchini, tomato, onion, red pepper, butter, and eggs. I took half of it, put it on a large roll, and cut it in three pieces to eat the next day for breakfast and lunch. When I sat down to eat, I was unsure which was my glass of wine. No one claimed the one I thought was mine, so I sipped. The lady from the market came in, signed us up and took our 10 euro. I showed her my passport and my Camino credential and she stamped it with the special stamp of Valcarlos Municipal Albergue.

The collection of wine bottles on the table was growing. I hated to leave the group but I knew I needed sleep. I cleaned up and put on my sleep sack nighty. Grace saw me in the bunk room and said, "Woo!" I was worried and asked her if it looked okay or if it was too sheer. She smiled and said, "No, not at all, it's great." Someone closed the bunk room door and I put my sleep mask on and earplugs in and tried to sleep. At 1:45 am, I was still awake. My mind was racing, going over my experiences of the day. I was meeting so many new and fun people.

The next morning, I got up, dressed, and got ready to leave. Shirley made coffee. I was glad for a cup. The kitchen had toast, butter, and yogurt: food that I usually don't eat but I thought, *What the heck?* The experience of eating with others was attractive. I noticed that the table by the oven was entirely covered with wine bottles and glasses. No room for breakfast. I wondered where all the bottles came from. The mercado closed early. I guessed they were all prepared ahead of time.

I was militantly keeping my pack light and not taking anything extra. I guessed the young men with their big muscles could take more things than me easily.

I walked out and up the parking area and right before me was a wonderful colorful mural on a white wall that said Valcarlos in large letters and it had a picture of a pilgrim and some country scenery. What a send-off! I saw Terry taking pictures of it. We walked on together. We started on a path next to the river. Sheep were roving with short quick steps over a field on the steep hillside. It was glorious, walking by waterfalls and through a forest. The trail was uphill with close mountains on both sides. It was immense but intimate being so close to the hills with a little river babbling down below. Little bridges with rails kept us safe. Big trees with little leaves and shrubs hugged the trail and us as we passed. Even the air seemed green with the foliage all around, below, and up above.

Terry and I took each other's pictures. Then she said she wanted to stay there for a while and write. I was thinking about how far I had to go that day and I decided to leave her to her solitude and move on.

I met Samir and he told me we would have to go

to the road; because of the snow, the trail was too slippery. I followed him up to the road. He took off walking fast and I at my own pace. I watched ahead around the curvy road to see when a truck was going to pass. Then I faced away from the road when it passed. The vibration shook me but it was less scary turning my back to it. What a different environment! The black two-way road with trucks and cars whizzing by with a dirt cliff drop off on one side and a dirt mountain going up on the other side of the street. It was very stark. All around, I heard water draining down in little culverts on the sides of the road. It must have rained the night before. The wind whipped around intermittently separate from the wind created by the trucks.

I walked for hours on the road and then I saw Justin and Christina. They were on a trail off the road. They didn't get the memo that we needed to go to the road. I asked them if the trail was safe. They didn't know what I was talking about. I followed them into the woods again. I had had enough of the road. The trail was gooey mud. We passed patches of snow. Burr! The wind whipped through the canyon below. We crossed a stream stepping on rocks as the path led us farther uphill on the winding path through the trees. They walked on as I walked my pace. As the forest fell away, the mountain emerged stark with light snow on the ground. I could still see dirt and grass through the snow. It was cold. The trail fell away too and I could see a lookout at the barren top of the mountain with signs depicting the far-off mountains with names and descriptions of historic significance. Christina called me over to see the signs. She was excited to see the view. I just wanted to get warm.

Turning away from the view, I saw the monastery at Roncesvalles in the distance. I came in the arched doorway and into the warmth of the reception area. A smiling greeter pointed me to the check-in with a set-up of four queues. The building was clad in thick, light, honey-colored hardwood, as were the clerks' desks. When it was my turn, I showed my passports and paid for my bed, dinner, and breakfast. I was given a bed number paper and dinner card and shown the stairs. As I climbed to my floor, I started wondering if it would be a lower bunk. I was met at the top of the stairs by a helper who looked at my paper and led me to my bed. As I passed, I spied Diana in a bunk. I waved and kept following my leader past cubicle after cubicle with two wooden bunk beds in each. My bunk was the lower one on the left. Whew! I wondered if they automatically gave white-haired seniors lower bunks. I made a mental note to always ask for a lower bunk.

When I unpacked, everything in my pack felt cold. I took a warm shower and a nap before dinner. Our dinner location was listed on the colored card. I put it in my coin purse. The restaurants in town served us dinner. Our reservation was indicated on our card. At dinner time we were ushered out of the albergue and down the street. I showed my card at the first restaurant and was lucky it was the right one. Diane had a different restaurant. The waitress led me through the first full dining room to another that had deep rose-colored walls. I sat at a big round table and waited for more people to show up. There was wine on the table and I poured myself a glass. A couple sat at the table and Diane got a change of venue and joined us. There were two choices for dinner. I chose the chicken, rice, and vegetables, leery of fish in a landlocked location. The dinner was good. Diane said the fish was good too. Afterward, I went into the church. I was bummed that I missed the pilgrim's service. Another mental note: check to see when the pilgrim Mass is when I get to the albergue. The church had many beautiful statues of the Virgin Mary and St. James and the Pilgrim. Dramatically, the lighting was localized on each statue and didn't penetrate the darkness all around.

After dinner, I hit the hay, hoping for a quiet night and no snoring. The earplugs that I bought on Amazon, all the way from Germany, because they said they were the best in the world, didn't work at all. They were cotton and wax. The directions said not to put them down your ear canals, but to just have them on the inside of the outside of your ear. That didn't work at all. They fell out. I think the only way they would work is if you did put them down the ear canal. They probably couldn't say that in the directions incase someone somehow got injured from it.

I left Roncesvalles early with Diane. We were hiking to Zubiri, 22.3 km, much too far. It was a brisk morning. We took each other's pictures by the Roncesvalles sign. We walked in snow at first and then as we went along the snow disappeared. We passed a great fence made out of discarded odd pieces of gnarled wood held together with wire. In the first town, I wanted to stop at the bar and get a coffee and use the restroom. Diane was game but I noticed she didn't get anything and she didn't need to use the facilities. I felt bad to detain her, but she seemed alright with it and enjoyed talking to the proprietor. The many shells were displayed around town, such as on the sidewalk, and on an iron fence, and there were yellow arrows to follow too. A giant colorful mural was on a wall with "welcome" spelled in what seemed like every language. It felt great to be walking with Diane. Outside of town, we walked down a country road. An arrow told us to turn left at a fence. A forest thick with pine trees lay on our right and a field lay on our left. It began to rain softly in spite of the forecast saying it was supposed to be the only day that week with no rain. I guessed the forecasts weren't accurate on the Camino. In the next town, Diane decided to rest and told me to go on. Sadly, I took off on my own. I kept noticing hearts everywhere. The puddle on the street was shaped like a heart. Even a smeared dog doo was shaped like a heart. Really? There were heart-shaped rocks about every 10 feet. It made me feel like I was loved and think of those I loved. I wondered if they were gifts from my husband's spirit.

The mountains were brutal with many winding trails that went uphill. I would see what looked like the end of the uphill not far ahead only to get there and find the trail turned to show another uphill, only steeper. It went on again and again. Ugh, I reassured myself with the thought that it couldn't go on forever, there had to be an end to it at some point. I got into a cadence with my poles and breathing. Regular walking was breathing in six steps and out two. My uphill pace was four steps in and two out. Up steep hills, my breathing pattern was, two steps in and two out. When my feet hurt, I did Tai Chi walking, rolling my foot as I stepped and lifting my foot completely at the end of each step. When my feet still hurt, I walked on the outside of my foot and then on the inside of my foot. I was actively avoiding foot pain all day long. I got into a groove and just kept going. I had to go over some rocky downhills on my butt when I sort of fell (gracefully.) After I made it most of the way down the hill, Samir came by and tried to help me up. I didn't want to get up. I just continued to scooch on my bum instead, hoping I wouldn't make holes in my pants. The trail was made of striated layers of rock that were upended, uneven, and impossible for me to walk on. I was extra careful to not fall. I did want to complete the pilgrimage. I didn't care what it looked like. I wanted to be safe and not sorry. In the end, I was pleased that my pants had no holes.

I was so glad to see the sign for Zubiri. I had a reservation at an albergue there. Coming into town I crossed over a river with an ancient stone bridge. I looked into the windows of an albergue but didn't find anyone about. I kept walking. A passing girl asked me if I were looking for an albergue and told me to keep walking, as there was one further down. The town had some really big factory-like buildings with angular graphics on the high walls. Hardly anyone was around. I passed a bus stop where a couple was waiting on a bench. When I got to the albergue, I went in. A woman brought me a complimentary beer. Really? She told me to leave my boots on the rack, they were so wet and muddy, and my poles in the bin.

There was a basket of newspaper and she told me to crumple it up and stuff my boots with it to get them to dry. I gave her 15 euro for my bed and breakfast. She asked me if I wanted to have dinner there. I said yes and paid for that too. She showed me to my bunk. I found a locker with a USB port inside to charge my phone. She said to put a euro in the slot and pull the key out. Then when you put the key in again and turn it, you got your euro back. Some albergues had trouble with people stealing phones in the night while pilgrims slept. Not this place.

I cleaned up and took a nap. Only one other person wanted dinner at the albergue. The woman asked her boss if it were okay to make supper for just two people. She got the okay. She seemed happy to have her job extended for the day. She called us to come and eat. Samir and Daniel and some others were out on the patio eating nuts, chips and guacamole from the grocery store. My dinner partner was embarrassed as we sat down to eat. He told me that when he found out that it was just the two of us, he wished he hadn't said yes. He poured the wine. We looked at each other and having noticed his accent, I asked him where he was from. "Australia," and he was off, talking about his home and family. His wife left him, and he was lost without her. He just couldn't live his day-to-day life anymore. Someone suggested he go on the Camino to sort things out. He told me about a book he read called *Boots*. It was about an old woman who walked the Camino. She found heart-shaped rocks on the trail and gave them to people along the way. I told him that I was seeing so many heart-shaped rocks. I didn't pick them up because I wanted to leave them there so others could find them too. He smiled excitedly and told me I should pick them up and give them to people. I would make them feel special. We shared our stories as we ate a gourmet meal. It was amazingly enjoyable. After dinner, he took a little bag of shell charms out of his pocket and gave me one. He said he wanted me to have it to remember our dinner together. I slipped it onto my safety pin that had a couple of other medals and pinned it to my collar. I asked the cook when we had to be out in the morning. She said it didn't matter. When I pressed her, she said, "11 am."

When I woke the next morning, I was tired. Everyone else and their stuff were gone from the room.

The snoring during the night had been atrocious. I went down to the dining room and breakfast was in full swing. They had bread, butter, Nutella, yogurt, cocoa, and coffee. Samir was just finishing his coffee and ready to take off. After breakfast, I decided to take advantage of the quiet and got some more sleep. I packed up and laid down. After my nap, I went down and I grabbed the newspaper out of my somewhat drier boots, put them on, grabbed my sticks from the bin and left at 10:10 am. The door locked behind me.

CHAPTER 3

THE LADY AT THE MONASTERY

63 KM

Lots of rain and mud made me think of writing poetry about mud. I was busy walking, following the yellow arrows up into the clouds. It was misty and so fresh. Water streamed down ditches on the sides and under the trail, making music in the quiet with the chirping birds. I saw hearts everywhere, even a little puddle heart. I picked up a heart rock and then another, stuffing them in my pocket. After the mud, I encountered a more-sandy road edged by a log fence with a crisscross design. It was charming and the sand was easier to walk on. Then I came to the freeway, I wasn't looking forward to walking on the freeway again, but the arrow pointed to a tunnel under the freeway with lots of graffiti. It was really cool. I could see many pilgrims walking on a trail that followed above the freeway on a grassy area. Across the freeway was a giant natural escarpment of vertical striations of deep purple dirt and grey dirt. It was beautiful and made me think what a wonderful artist God is.

Walking over a stone bridge over the river and into Trinidad de Are, I found the monastery albergue, a large dark grey stone edifice. Walking down into the below-street-level entrance, I opened the ancient wooden door and got in line behind the other pilgrims. I was hoping there was a bunk for me too. A monk suggested I put my poles over in the bin with the rest. I was reluctant to leave the line. He said it would be okay. Then I noticed a bunch of chairs next to the line. He kindly told me to sit down and relax. I must have looked tired. We each moved up the line taking the chair vacated by the person in front of us. When it was my turn, I handed the man my passport and credential. He said it would be 8 euros for the night. A group of us were escorted out and across the garden and up the stone stairs to the bunkhouse. He took us into the kitchen, told us to put coins into a box if we used the washer and clean up after ourselves in the kitchen, and he showed us where the bathrooms were.

There were maybe 40 bunk beds. The main room was for the men and there was a smaller side room for the women. Clothes were hung to dry on hooks on the wall. I found a lower bunk, laid out my sleeping bag, and put my pack on the chair. I laid down and fell asleep immediately.

When I woke, I went out to find a grocery store. Searching around the store for what to eat for dinner, I got eggs, zucchini, a big red pepper, onion, cheese, bread, butter, and a small unfrosted cake. I didn't get the strawberries because they looked beat up.

When I got back to the monastery, pilgrims were in the kitchen making dinner together and individual-ly. I met a couple from Hungary, a lady from Holland, who was walking with her injured friend, a couple of guys from Cuba, one from Spain, and Samir from LA.

I talked with a lady from Kuala Lumpur who had a cast on her broken arm. She said that she fell in the shower. The monastery was letting her stay there till she healed. She had been there for more than a week. Wow, that cemented my resolve to be very careful and not get into a situation where I might fall. I wore my shower shoes in every shower. It didn't matter if the shower shoes made it difficult to wash my feet.

I told the group that I hoped they would have cake with me for my mother's birthday. One of the ladies and the couple said they would. I cut the cake and put it in the middle of the rough wooden table. Samir said he would eat some for breakfast if there were some left.

The lady from Holland said, "You must have a very special relationship with your mom." I sighed and said, "No." She said, "You're celebrating her birthday." I sighed again and said, "Yes, it's the first one since she died. We always celebrated her birthday." It felt right to celebrate.

She said, "Yeah, I didn't have a good relationship with my mom either." She looked sad and perhaps relieved that we had comradery in this. We want to have a good experience with our mom. Maybe we hope that someone else does. If not, we have solidarity over it.

I made my dinner. It was so simple. Cut up and fry the onion, pepper, and zucchini in butter, scramble eggs in a bowl and pour it over the fried veggies. There were a few spices and salt available in the kitchen. It was ready to eat in no time. The Amsterdam lady told me she was watching me to see how I was cooking. I was surprised because it seemed so basic to me. We sat down across from each other and I guessed she had already eaten. We got to talking as pilgrims will. I was excited to tell her the story I had formulated, hoping it wasn't too weird for her.

"I believe that before I incarnated into our world, I was a low vibrational spirit with God, out in the universe. I found out that being a human it was possible to raise my vibration because humans can have unconditional love. That's why I decided to be born into this world even knowing what trouble I would attract because of my low vibration. And I did attract trouble. When going for unconditional love, you must have adversity. It's easy to love those who are nice to us but our tormentors require unconditional love from us.

So, the adversity was attracted and part of the cure."

I told her about how I had been trying to raise my vibration over the years. But when I learned about Ho'oponopono, my life changed forever. I looked it up on the internet and found many teachers of Ho'oponopono. I learned that it was about raising your vibration. I started using the prayer to clear my energy and separate my connection to difficult people and situations.

I told her about how I was on vacation with my husband and I felt so sad. I wanted to be happy. Lying in bed at night, I repeated the prayer to myself, "I Love you. I'm sorry. Please forgive me. Thank you. I love you

Then I tried the long version, "I love you, I love God, God loves me, God loves the other person, the other person loves God, I love the other person, the other person loves me. I'm sorry this situation happened or exists. Please forgive me for whatever is going on in me that caused me to attract this. Thank you for showing me this so I could heal. I love you, I love God, God loves me, God loves the other person, the other person loves God, I love the other person, the other person loves me."

I realized that it was making me feel worse. I felt shame and guilt when I said I was sorry, and please forgive me. I knew this wasn't what Ho'oponopono was about. It wasn't about shame. I realized I must be doing it wrong. I felt the heaviness on my heart and the sadness on my face. So, I changed it up a bit. When I said please forgive me, I added I forgive me and I forgive it up. When I did this, I felt a giant re-frigerator-sized sadness come out of my heart and up and away from me. I sent it out into the universe. Then I said, thank you for showing me this so I could heal, and I felt washed and so clean. It was gone and I hadn't known what was making me sad but now it was out of me. Oh my, I was so happy. As I lay there, different painful memories from my past came up like they always did when I couldn't get to sleep. I used my extended Ho'oponopono on them too. I was awake all night doing this. I got really tired and asked the angels to come and help me to get these memories and feelings out. It was like the sadness went deep in-side of me even to the beginning of time. I had no idea how to loosen them so deeply so I asked the angels to help me get them out. When morning came, I felt a lot of clearing. I was tired but elated and happy.

The Dutch woman was smiling and asked me to write down the Ho'oponopono prayer. I did and gave it to her.

I noticed that the Hungarian woman had bought the beat-up strawberries. She washed them and they were dripping juice. She took two pieces of my mother's birthday cake and she covered them with her very juicy strawberries it looked delicious. She looked happy as she handed one to her husband. I told her that my grandmother was from Hungary and I loved everything Hungarian. I also told her that I had a cousin in Hungary. I was a friend of his on Facebook. I told her that he was a football or soccer player and he posted on Facebook a TV sports interview he was in. I didn't know if he were famous or not. The husband asked me what his name was. I told him, Zoltan Lang. His eyes got big and he said that he had heard of my cousin and that he was a very good player. How nice.

Soon it was almost time for lights out. The ladies' and men's bathrooms were separate. The showers were behind tall wooden doors. There was an anteroom in each and two hooks to hang clothing. I took my bar of soap, towel, sleep sack nighty, and shower shoes in. The water was plentiful and warm. I used the lightweight washcloth the flight attendant handed out before dinner on my flight to Paris. It served me well most of the Camino until I forgot and left it behind. My towel was small and thin but it worked just fine to dry me off.

When I got to bed, I learned that the ladies from Holland were going home the next day. The lady I talked to said that she had already walked the Camino and she was just there for her friend who could no longer walk because of knee problems. I told her I had a cure for knee problems. She said no, her friend wanted to go home. I guessed that it wasn't such a big deal for them to go home since Holland isn't as far away as the USA.

I was so tired. The lady from Holland suggested that I sleep in and have a leisurely breakfast and not rush in the morning. The guy who checked us in didn't tell us we had to be out at any special time. I thought that was a good idea. I somehow got to sleep that night, probably because I was overtired.

In the morning, I got up a little late. I went into

the kitchen and started preparing my breakfast. I was happy to notice that the cake was almost gone and there was more food on the table to share too, from people lightening their packs. I cooked more of the same as I had for dinner. First, I cooked my breakfast. The man who checked us in came in and seemed upset that we were still there. The others were almost done and left right away. The lady from Kuala Lumpur was there sitting at the table. I just smiled at the man and he went out. After I ate my breakfast, I started cooking my lunch and I put it on a large roll with cheese. He came in, eyes bulging in obvious disbelief, and he commenced to yell at me in Spanish. I quietly finished what I was doing. He found his English words and told me angrily that I was stealing his day from him. I offered to pay him more and he said my money wouldn't pay for the loss of his day. So, I finished up and got my stuff. I tried to go to the bathroom before I left, but he was standing in the doorway with the mop and broom in an x behind him and he said, "No, go." And he pointed to the door. I was trying to imagine leaving without peeing. Then he yelled and chased me out the door. I roughly threw the pack over my shoulder, opened the door, and walked quickly and carefully down the stairs. The lady with the broken arm was in the garden. She told me to just go. I told her I didn't know where the exit door was. She took me to the entry room where there was a bathroom. When I got out of the bathroom, the formerly angry man was standing there looking at me. He had a sad look on his face. He handed me my medals on a safety pin that had been ripped off my collar when I slung my pack on. One of my medals was missing. It was St. Jerome. I asked, "Where's St. Jerome?" He repeated, "St. Jerome" and ran out into the garden to look on the walk and in the grass. I looked too. We did not find it. I said that I guessed St. Jerome was for someone else. When I left, he still looked sad.

CHAPTER 4

THE WAY TO CIZUR MENOR

73 KM

I walked by the big town of Pamplona. I was thinking of staying there the night but for some reason, I
wanted to keep going when I got there, so I kept walking on the path over rolling hills, and pretty much
flat terrain. I was quite tired when I arrived at a park.
There was a bench, so I sat down and put my pack
next to me. I watched a couple holding hands walking
on the path and the birds playfully chirping and flying from tree to tree. A young man (I assumed it was

an angel) came up to me and asked me if I was looking for an albergue. It was music to my ears! He pointed up the hill behind me and told me where there was a place to stay. I jumped up with new energy, thanked him, and went to investigate.

The sign on the albergue said Mirabel Roncal. Wow, one of my guardian angels is named Marybell and Ron was my husband. I decided I was there by divine appointment. It was a large low whitewashed building. There was a window with a ledge like a pay booth but no one was there. I walked through the gate and a woman walked out of the office. I asked her if I could have a bunk for the night. She said to come in. I asked her about the name of their albergue. She said that her name was Mirabel and her sister was Ronda. It was their parents' place, but they were in charge now. How nice. I gave her my passport and credential. She recorded what she needed and stamped my pilgrim credential. The albergue was a bunch of bunkhouses, a dining room/kitchen, and washrooms surrounding a large grassy area where there were a lot of patio tables and chairs. Some tables were on the cement walk area in front of the rooms and others were out on the grass.

As she led me to a bunk room, she told me the rules of clothes washing, bathroom, and eating. We were all supposed to eat at the restaurant in town across from the park. The pilgrim meal was 10 euro and we could go at 5 pm or 7 pm but we must make a reservation. There was a lower bunk available. I laid out my sleeping bag but I kept hitting my head on the low bunk above, so I moved to the top bunk.

I was surprised to see Christina from Valcarlos sitting on a top bunk across the room. I thought I wouldn't see her and her brother again since they were young and obviously would walk faster than me. Christina told me she had blisters and couldn't walk fast. Wow, that was too bad! She said they were doing laundry and asked me if I would like to do some with them. I said yes, I had a few things to wash. I went with her to the washing room which was in the room at the entrance to the men's restroom! Mirabel told me with a big smile that they set it up that way to emphasize that washing wasn't women's work and to encourage the men to do the wash. She suggested that I hang my clothes under the covered patio since it was supposed to rain. It was fairly windy so I supposed the clothes would dry quickly. When the clothes were washed, I took them to the patio and the clothesline was full of clothes. I found some little spaces and hung my clothes in between the others. I went down to the restaurant and made my reservation for 7 pm. They gave me a card with my time and restaurant info on it. Back at the albergue, I sat down at a table on the patio to write my Facebook entry. An older man came into the patio and indicated that I should move to another area. He said, "Caballos, Caballos!" Then he opened the giant double gate at the outside of the patio. I was surprised to see a busy road right next to the quiet peaceful patio. After a while, in trod three horses, two with riders. One rider was a beautiful Spanish woman with a long green skirt and a long-sleeved golden yellow blouse and riding boots. The other rider wore pants and cowboy boots she was leading the third horse holding a rope. The riders looked happy but weary. The man led them away and I didn't see them anymore.

I saw Christina sitting at a table in the yard. I told her that I would like them to visit me sometime in San Diego because I had some pullout couches and they would be welcome. I gave her my phone number. She asked me if I was on the WhatsApp group from Valcarlos. I said no. She said she would send a message off to Daniel and ask him to put me on it. She asked me if I would eat with them. I said yes and asked what I could bring. She said nothing because they had too much food and would probably have to throw it away if I didn't eat with them so, they would love to share it with me, besides, Justin carried a lot of food in his pack and they needed to lighten his pack. I told her I would wash the dishes. She said that they would love to visit me in San Diego and it would all be good. I called the restaurant to cancel my reservation. The lady didn't speak English. I hoped she got the message correctly.

In the evening I went into the kitchen. The angel guy who rescued me from the park and told me about Mirabel Roncal was boiling water in a big pot to make spaghetti. Justin was opening a can of colorful mixed beans to eat with it. I was glad that I would get to meet my angel and I would be eating with them all. Justin was cutting up some salami to put into the spaghetti too. I set the table. We sat down in the dining room. Justin had a carton of milk for us to drink with our dinner. It was such a treat to experience eating dinner the way they designed it especially since I have always been the food arranger in my family. Most of it was food that I don't usually eat, but I ate with relish and enjoyed myself. We spoke about our families and our lives. I told them about my negative ion clothes that keep me well. I thought the reason I didn't get blisters was because of my negative ion socks that had two layers and they wicked moisture away from my skin

After I washed the dishes, I got ready for bed. It was great to have a really nice bright lady's room. Everything was well thought out, clean, and neat. The colors were yellow and white. There were even a couple of bowls below the soap dispensers to catch soap that might leave a gooey drip residue.

There was a lot of activity in the bunk room. A lot of English was being spoken. There were people from Canada, Holland, Cuba, England, Norway, and more. I noticed that Christina was already in bed with her beanie pulled down over her eyes. I thought that was a great idea. I had a sleep mask from the Paris flight, but the beanie was better. I got out my red negative ion beanie and put my earplugs in, pulled the beanie down over my eyes and tried to sleep. I hoped the last person in bed would turn out the light.

The next day was very special. I was getting so strong the hills didn't bother me. I was glad to walk up a big hill with a rocky path to an area where giant statues were cut out of sheet metal. They depicted pilgrims with long staffs. I asked someone to take my picture. The path down was rocky also. It wasn't winding but went straight down. A caring man told me that he was worried I would fall and he asked me to take off my sunglasses so I could see better. I told him that I could see just fine and that I needed my sunglasses so I wouldn't get cataracts. He said he understood that but he was worried that my glasses were so dark that I would stumble on the rocks. It was amazing to experience the care pilgrims have for each other.

Walking up a hill near Uterga, I came to a beautiful statue in a park called the Virgin of Irunbidea. I sat on a bench and said my rosary. I went into the town to get a café con leche and use the restroom. I met a man on the road who suggested that I stay at the Albergue Casa Baztán. I was the first one there. The reception room was quite bohemian and artsy, with deep maroon and blue tapestries, and a mosaic with mirror pieces. After I gave him my papers, the young man checked me in and stamped my credential. I paid for my bunk and dinner and breakfast. I selected a bottom bunk near the middle of the room. He also showed me a bedroom with a large bed saying it had a private bath. I said no thank you. I decided to take a shower right away since the bathroom was coed. When I got out of the shower, an attractive Spanish couple had arrived and was setting up at the far end of the room. The man immediately laid down on the top bunk and went to sleep. Good idea to sleep when there's no snoring. Soon, another couple came in and took a bunk bed near the door. The beds slowly got filled as the afternoon went on. No one took the private room. The other couple was from the USA. They were a very tall older man and a middle-aged very cute woman. The woman was having trouble with her boots being too small. She arranged for the proprietor to take her back to Pamplona to the Decathlon store to get some better boots. The man was carrying a lot of beauty paraphernalia for her: a curling iron, a bag of cosmetics, and hairdryer. I told her that if he wanted her to be beautiful that it was good that he was carrying all of that for her.

When we went in to dinner, a man was sitting at the table deep in conversation with the Spanish man. He had decided to not get dinner. Our cook invited him to leave the table to eat his food from his pack elsewhere. I watched the Spanish woman to see how she ate her bread. She was very slim. Bread made me fat. She took a piece of bread, without butter. When she finished eating, she still had half of her piece of bread uneaten and left on her plate. What a revelation! Bread is always eaten, but not much by thin people. I loved bread and butter so much, I ate many pieces at dinner. Eating bread made my middle, ankles, and feet swell. If I kept eating it, I wouldn't be able to zip up my sleeping bag. The conversation around the table was informative. The Spanish man had finished the Camino two weeks earlier with his friends. His wife decided to go too and he didn't want her to go alone. He told us to watch out around Villa Major. There was a steep hilly alternative route. He recommended that we not take it, as it was brutal and he wished he hadn't taken it.

The next day, I walked 29 km or about 18 miles! My plan to walk 10 miles a day or about 16 km and be done by 2 pm was foiled because every albergue in every town that I went to was either closed or full. So, I kept walking. I planned to be at Cirauqui by 2 pm. The town had a big sign advertising its albergue and I found it up a perilous path. I got there at 2:30 pm. My book said it would be opened by April 1, but it was closed. On the way back down to the road, I noticed another easier path, thank God. I continued to Lorca. They were full. I walked to Villatuerta and they were closed because they hadn't received some of their supplies. He said he was sorry and asked me if I wanted him to call me a cab. I said no. I went to a restaurant. They also wanted to call me a cab. I must have looked really tired. A man having coffee at the restaurant made a call and told me that Estella was one hour further and they were open. I got to Estella around 6:30 pm. The lady said she had a bed for me. I gave her my papers and she checked me in and stamped my Camino credential. As we walked through the kitchen I saw Shirley from Valcarlos. I followed the lady out through the garden patio to a ground level room already populated with an Italian men's biking club. I put my things down and laid out my bag. When I went back to the kitchen to see Shirley, I saw Samir in the garden. Shirley was making dinner with her new friend, Rocky from Australia. They fed me pasta with pesto and told me to rest. Whew, my feet hurt! It was too much walking for me. One good thing about having to walk so far was that I caught up with Shirley and Samir, and I saw Terry at breakfast the next day.

The bathroom was small and coed. There were red yellow and blue painted doors on three showers. While I was showering, one of the bikers came in and took a shower in the stall next to mine I could see his hairy legs and bare feet. I brushed my teeth at the small sink and went to my bed. I hung my laundry around my bed with my small clothesline. It was hopefully like a privacy screen. The men were respectful but they snored loudly all night long, ugh. At breakfast in the morning, there were a lot of packages of donuts, pound cake, and bread on the table that others left behind. I made myself a giant sandwich with cheese, salami, butter, and sliced tomato. I cut it into three pieces. I left by myself and stopped at the first bar to get some café con leche and use their powder room. The day's walk was pleasant. I walked by a colorful royal blue, purple, and red playground for adults and kids. It had interesting exercise equipment for adults and a jungle gym and slide for kids. I walked by a wonderful painting of a dove with wings spread accompanied by a clock and flowers on the wall at the top of the house.

Walking through the countryside past vineyards and fields, I started watching for a place to pee. I was walking by a rocky mountain with trees and foliage all around. I saw a big boulder a little off the trail. No one was around. So, I pulled 'em down and sat back hanging my butt over the back side of the rock. I commenced peeing. Oh no, I saw a man walking up. I pulled my scarf up to cover me and grabbed a sandwich out of my bag and started eating it. I smiled at him as he walked by. He said, "Oh, I thought you were taking a pee." I smiled and said, "I am." He laughed and said, "Well, thank you for that moment." Then he left. Sheesh! I tried to get up before anyone else came by. The bushes around me had stickers and they grabbed me as I tried to get up. I pulled away harder and pulled up my pants fast. As I walked away, I could feel stuff in my pants jostling around. Note to self: when you hang yourself over a rock in the woods for a wee, scrape off the twigs, rocks, leaves, dried berries, and moss before you hoist up your knickers. It was all because I didn't want to try out my SheeWee, a device for women to pee standing up. At home, I watched the video and I successfully tried it in the shower. I just couldn't go there in my mind on the Camino. I met a lady from Colorado who had a different brand of ladies' peeing device, and she said she used it.

The trail became wide and had yellow arrows on blue background signs to follow through the maze of fields. Off in the distance, I saw a lone sentinel obelisk keeping watch over the field. I saw a carefully sculpted field planted around a wildly growing hilltop.

I met with Justin at Irache, a vineyard that had a dual fountain for pilgrims. One spigot was for wine and the other was for water. I got my cup out of my pack and poured myself some wine. I had someone take my picture with Justin in front of the fountain.

Later on, I walked across an arched bridge over a wildly raging waterfall before a town. I followed the arrows, which led to steep rocky disheveled steps next to a stone wall. I made it to Villamayor de Monjardín around noon. They did not open for 2 hours. I sat down out in front of a large church-looking building at a table and chairs. A man was there too, he came and sat down. He said he needed a rest. He was sad that the albergue wasn't a restaurant and not open yet. He said he was looking for a restaurant because he wanted to be served. There was no restaurant in the town. We sat and talked for a while. He was Craig from Oregon. I told him how tired I was because of the snoring in the albergues. He wanted to know why I was staying in the albergues. He said we were older and didn't need to do the Camino on the cheap. He said I could get a private room and have a good night's sleep. I told him I was remodeling my kitchen when I got home and any money I saved could go into my kitchen. Craig said he was getting hungry. I reached into my pack and pulled out two of my sandwiches. I gave him one. He thanked me and said it was a perfect meal. I told him that I was 69 years old and I was going to have my 70th birthday on the Camino. He thought that was great. He said that he hadn't considered that he would be doing this sort of thing in his 70s. I gave him hope.

Pretty soon, a young lady came out of the albergue and asked us if we would like some tea. Craig made his goodbyes and took off. I was surprised to see Samir walk up to the albergue. A man in town told him there was a trail up the mountain above the town and he decided to walk up to see the view. Good for him for wanting to do extra walking. After the young lady brought me some tea, she asked me if I would like a foot bath. Oh my, I said, "yes." She suggested that I bring my tea out of the wind and into the peregrino room where she would bring me my foot bath. The room had a wooden couch and chairs. The pillows on the couch were home-made of delightful old blue and red flowered material and blue and white gingham. It reminded me of my Aunt Gertie's house in the mountains near home. There was a hot pot, cups, and tea on a cart and a jar to put coins in for the tea. I soaked my feet in the warm water, lovely. At 2 pm, they started to check pilgrims in out on the patio. I made sure I got close to the beginning of the line. The blond man checking people in said they were all volunteers and missionaries for their church in Holland. Their church sponsored this albergue on the Camino.

He took my passport and credential. He signed me in and gave me my stamp. I paid for my bunk and dinner and breakfast. He said there was a mercado down in town. It would be open at 5 pm. A missionary took me upstairs to the bunk room where I claimed my lower bunk. I went out on the roof patio where there were a sink and stacks of pastel colored bowls. I washed my clothes with my bar soap and rinsed them. I brought my bowl of clothes down to the blond man who had a centrifuge. Yay! Then I hung my clothes on the wooden racks on the patio out front with my safety pins to hold them on. I went up to my bunk and fell asleep. When I woke up, I took a shower in the large bathroom, I found the twigs, moss, rocks, and berries in my tights. The pale wooden showers had very interesting and large closure devices. The shower was good, warm, and plentiful.

After I got dressed, I went down to the store. I was looking for a nail file because one of my fingernails was catching on things. I found a little kit with some emery boards, good enough. They had a package of soft camembert cheese, so I got it and salami, a tomato, and a big roll to make tomorrow's sandwich to go.

I also got a potato to nuke in the morning to keep me warm and then to eat, along with a cucumber and an apple.

Dinner at the albergue was quite a production. The dining room was filled with pilgrims. Everyone seemed happy and were talking. I sat down in the middle of one of the tables facing the kitchen, which was opened to the dining room. The chef and several missionaries were bustling around preparing dishes. There was soup first and many other dishes of chicken and vegetables and a big salad. They had my food! We were cautioned to take a little at first to make sure there was food for everyone. I ate my fill as the evening progressed. The conversation was light and enjoyable.

After dinner, we were invited into the meditation room. Sitting around on pillows on the floor, there was an inspiring lecture, followed by a meditation to beautiful music and then sharing. When it was over, we all lazed there peacefully, not wanting to leave. The tall blond man seemed to be trying to get us to leave with his little English.

I went up to bed. Samir was in a bunk across the room. In the morning, he was angry because of so much loud snoring. I asked him if I had been snoring. He said that my little snoring didn't bother him at all, but the loud snoring kept him awake. Yikes, I snored!

CHAPTER 5

PALM SUNDAY

135 KM

After missing Mass the Sunday before, I decided that I had to spend Saturday and Sunday night at a hotel each week. Usually, when I got into a town, I checked in and fell asleep. Then I wouldn't find out where Mass was and I would miss it. I was on a holy pilgrimage, after all. I wanted to go to Mass at least on Sunday. I was in Los Arcos for Saturday and Palm Sunday. The hotel, Albergue de Abuelita, was an albergue/hotel. I got there a little early so I went looking for the church. I came back at 2 pm and got my room for two nights and dinner both days and breakfasts, then got my credential stamped. The guy who checked me in said the procession would be in the morning and there would be a concert that evening. Dinner would be early, at 6 pm, in case anyone wanted to go to the concert at the church. I surely did. There was a bunk room on the first floor. My room was on the third floor, but it was actually the fourth floor if you're an American since we consider the ground floor to be the first floor. My ceiling was the wooden rafters under the roof. The room was freshly painted white and the furniture matched the wood tone of the rafters. A stylish grey and white duvet covered the bed. The windows had many small panes. The view out the window was of the wide blue sky and other roofs, or the tops of people's heads looking down below. It was perfect for me, solitude. I went back down to the church to find out when the Palm Sunday services were and where. A sign on the door said that there would be a procession starting at the Plaza of St. Frances on Sunday at 12:30 pm. I asked around where the plaza of St. Frances was, but couldn't successfully communicate with anyone. The proprietor of the albergue told me that it was two streets over to the right, out the front door.

Dinner was family-style at the big table in the dining room/kitchen. We ate lentil soup and bread. I felt shy, not knowing anyone. The man next to me said he wanted my opinion of marriage. He thought that it was a 50/50 arrangement. I told him that I found that it was a 100/100 arrangement. I told him that people who give their marriage just 50 % are not really committed. He was intrigued. Sadly, his marriage failed. I left dinner early to get to the concert. I was surprised that I was the only one who wanted to go. The concert was divine and it was inspiring to be in the church at night with the families of the town. I sat in an area where a lot of single older women sat. I supposed we were the widows, and I felt like I belonged.

Sunday morning breakfast was unfrosted yellow cake, cereal, yogurt, and hard-boiled eggs. I put the yogurt and the cereal together, put it in the microwave and had an egg with it. It was great. I went upstairs, did my laundry in the bathroom sink, and hung it around my room on my clothesline.

I went out to find the Plaza de San Francisco. I

walked to the right and came to a row of houses so I had to turn. I hoped left was the right way. I asked someone who didn't know what I was talking about. I turned right next and continued to a plaza where people were gathering. I found it! A truck arrived with a load of branches from different kinds of trees. He unloaded them in a pile on the side of the plaza. People went over and got one or two branches. I grabbed an olive branch. Some men in bright green robes arrived, and a beautiful bigger than life-sized statue of Christ on a donkey holding a giant palm branch on a wheeled litter showed up.

The procession lined up behind the priest who was leading the singing and three men in black and green robes were behind him. The man in the middle was carrying a large cross and the two others were carrying lanterns on poles. The litter was carried along by the men in green robes. Many of the children were dressed like people from Jesus' time. I recognized a few families from church the night before. I walked along with them. We walked through the town, the crowd filling the narrow streets. People stood on balconies and in doorways to watch the procession.

We ended up at the church. Inside, the giant golden façade around the altar looked immense in the celebration. After a short ceremony, everyone dispersed.

It was lunchtime. I went into the bar and stood in a long line to get some food. I had a hard time getting attention. Finally, a person behind the bar asked me what I wanted. I pointed to a plate with crispy pork belly, another one with paella and a bottle of peach juice. The man said to go outside and sit at a table. I realized that only the men who wanted a drink stood in line and they didn't appreciate me being there. I sat at a table on the plaza in front of the church and the waitress brought me my food. It was a very social environment on the plaza. Many families and groups of friends in lovely clothes were eating together, talking, and laughing at tables on the plaza. I was there in my hiking boots and pilgrim attire, as were a few others. After I ate, I took a walk around the town. I stayed away from a large building's many dark hallways. No shops were opened on Sunday. The raging river defined the edge of the town.

The next morning, I heard at breakfast that Notre Dame Cathedral burned. Oh my gosh, I was just there a couple of weeks before when I was in Paris. I had gone to Mass at Notre Dame and had breakfast at a café across the street. Shocking. There was a new crew of pilgrims at breakfast Monday morning. I asked the group if anyone could figure out why my Bluetooth headphones wouldn't work. The young guy across from me took them and studied them carefully. He told me I had to close out the connection and reinstate it each time I turned them on. That was great to know; I thanked him. A young lady was having knee issues and said she would have to go home if they didn't get better. I told her about the cure my husband used as a runner. Take a bandana and tie it around the leg below the knee across the patella. She said she had a bandana and would try it. The breakfast was the same as the day before. I loved it.

On the road walking again, I reluctantly left Los Arcos, but I was drawn on by the adventure before me. The road was uphill with another trail uphill after that. Most of the day's walk wasn't difficult, as it traversed a flat area. I walked through a national park so I could use their restroom. I met a lady, Connie, from Wyoming. We walked through many towns together. It seemed there were about 2 km or less between towns. I stopped in one town at a farmacia and bought an ace bandage because my ankle was hurting. Out on the trail, there were big bushes of beautiful pink flowers that reminded me of the heather in Scotland. More pink flowers looked like apple blossoms on trees by the trail. Fields stretched out as far as we could see. We walked by a lot of irrigation terminals and over bridges across ditches for irrigation.

Connie showed me how to pee against a wall. Now I understood why they had so many rest areas with a giant wall behind them. You just pull em down and lean against the wall with your backside hold your knickers out of the way, and let go of it. Simple and fast. If you have some toilet paper and a zip bag to put it in, all the better. Problem solved. We talked and talked about our lives. She had a brother-in-law who had Parkinson's disease. I told her about my husband's experience with the disease. She was interested and asked many questions, gathering info to tell her sister. We walked under freeways, and out into the countryside under impossibly beautiful cloud-striated skies. We saw a colorful tiled picture of the Virgin Mary with the legend, "Nuestra Senora del Popo, Bendice al Pueblo de Bargota, protégé a los peregrinos," on a rock wall. In English, it means, "Our Lady of Popo, Bless the People of Bargota, protect the pilgrims." I loved these surprising colorful visual treats. Each town had a tall church which was the first thing we saw as we approached. Near the town of Viana, in the tunnel of an underpass, there was a big turquoise and dark blue picture of a shell painted with spray paint. It was really cool.

We finally came to a passage way that had a sign above it: Logrono, Ciudad del Camino. We were both planning to stay there. She seemed to know which albergue she wanted to stay at. We searched where we thought it was, but didn't find it. I showed the address to a lady in a candy shop. She asked one of her customers if he would show us where it was. He took us right to it. People along the Camino seem to feel a responsibility to get pilgrims where they needed to be.

We went into the building and there was no sign of an albergue. Connie asked a lady who pointed to the stairs. We went up and up and came to a door bell. Connie rang the bell and a man came, let us in, and led us to his wife, who stamped our credentials, recorded us and took our money. There was a refrigerator to store our food but not much else in the kitchen and no meals. If we had laundry, we could bring it to her and she would wash it for 5 euro. She showed us to our room and gave us a key. She told us to put the key in the box by the door when we left the next day. The room had 6 bunk beds. Only ladies stayed in our room. There was a men's bunk room down the hall. I immediately laid down and took a nap. Connie took her shower. After I took my shower, I gathered my laundry and gave it to the lady. I told her not to dry it. She said to come back in an hour. When I came back, she rescued my clothes from the dryer where her husband had put them. They were hot. If I dry my negative ion socks and underwear with heat, they shrink. Thankfully they weren't in the dryer long. I hung them out on the balcony to dry. It was windy out there which was good. Smells of fried foods wafted up from below. I hoped my clothes didn't take on the smell.

We went out and tried to find a sports bra. I left one of mine at a previous albergue. I was getting a complex because no one had one my size. I asked a shop keeper, "No tiene mujeres grandes en España?" Finally, I found a store that had one that didn't fit very well. I asked the sales lady to help me. She tugged here and there and, all of a sudden, it fit me. It was 54 euro! That was a lot. One thing I was learning on the Camino was how to take care of myself and get my needs met. We bought some fast food and Connie got orange juice.

When we got back to the room, all the beds were full. There were four young women who were talking and giggling. They were planning a night out on the town. I dreaded when they would get back and wake us up in the middle of the night. Actually, I slept all night. No one snored and the girls were miraculously quiet when they came in and didn't wake anyone. I asked one of the girls what time they got in, and she said they got in around 2. They tiptoed, and, even though they were tipsy, they got in bed without noise. Marvelous.

CHAPTER 6

HOLY WEEK

180 KM

I came into Navarrete through the rain. The Albergue La Casa del Peregrine, was halfway up a hill and set back on a switchback winding street. The building was the same color as the dirt ground and the hill behind it. A curtain hung across the door made of many hanging nylon ropes. I smiled and thought, *I want one of those.* It looked so cool. Inside were a large table and a rudimentary kitchen on the back wall. An Asian man took my passport and credential. I paid for my bunk, dinner, and breakfast. He led me upstairs. I was the only one there. I took off my ace bandage. The arch of my foot was hurting. I decided to wrap it differently the next day. I took a nap. When I woke, another Asian pilgrim was on the other side of the bunk room. I took my shower in the rickety shower stall, washed some clothes, and hung them around my bunk. I went out to find the church and find out what was on the agenda the first night of Holy Week.

The church wasn't far away. There would be a procession later in the evening. When I returned, it was time for a dinner of soup and pasta. I met a young South Korean woman, Kiko, at dinner. She said she wanted to go to the procession with me. She showed me her earrings that were shaped like a cross. Kiko told me that she was interested in Jesus. She asked me if I was Christian. I said yes and told her I was Catholic Christian. I checked with the proprietor to make sure I could get into the albergue after the church services. He said he would be there till 10. After dinner, we went to the plaza in front of the church. The most amazing spectacle I had ever seen was gathering there. There were droves of men in black or purple satin clothing with tall cone-shaped hats and face coverings. Each man had a drum and drum sticks. They were lining up in two lines next to each other with leaders getting their attention and giving directions. One man was carrying a banner that said, "Banda De Trompetas y Tambores." They played their drums for a while and stopped abruptly all together, following the leader's direction. There was a buzz of excitement among the onlookers and the drummers. The bells on the church rang to announce the beginning of the procession. First came the drummers, then a row of men playing a melody with whistles. Then the congregation followed. We walked through the town's narrow streets. At one point, half of the drummers went one way and the others went the other way with the procession following the second group. When we got back to the church, I was recording a video on my phone. An older man came up to me and pointed to the end of the street down below the plaza. The statue of The Sorrowful Virgin Mary in a beautiful black and gold embroidered dress was coming from the right. A statue of Jesus carrying the cross was coming from the other direction. All this time, the drums were getting louder and faster. Then they stopped abruptly as Mary saw her son. It was breathtakingly dramatic. I couldn't believe what I was seeing. I told Kiko I had never seen anything like that before. She nodded.

Kiko was worried about going into the church because she didn't have proper shoes. I showed her my shower shoes and said I was going to wear them into the church. She left and went to a youth gathering down below the plaza. I went into the church where they finished up the evening with a benediction. I hurried back to my albergue alone, hoping to get there before they locked the door. I made it.

After a good breakfast of scrambled eggs and bread, I left Navarrete and after walking all morning, I made it to Najera. I spent the rest of Holy Week there in my own room in a hotel. It was good that I had a reservation because there were no more rooms in town. Finding the hotel was very strange. The address was for a hotel that was closed. I called the number and the woman directed me to go to another hotel to check-in. I asked a man on the street where the address was and he said there were no more rooms. I said I had a reservation. He asked me my name then took me to the hotel where I checked in. I gave the lady my papers. She said one night. I said no, I was staying till Monday. Her eyes got wide and she looked at the man. I said, "This is a hotel, right? I can stay more than one night? When I made my reservation, I made sure I would be here all week. I'm staying for Holy Week." The man made an explanation in Spanish; and she agreed and said, "Okay." I asked her what time the service at the church was that evening. She said 6 pm. The room was on the third floor (but really on the fourth floor), and they had no elevator. I was just tired enough to want to not go downstairs again for a while. I had mud on my clothes from the rain and trail. I ate out of my backpack and took a nap. When I awoke, I took a shower and dressed in my clean pilgrim clothes for church.

The ceremony that evening was very similar to the one in Navarrete. It had drummers wearing purple satin robes without the headgear and with a little less drama. I sat with the pilgrims in the church. On the way out the door, a couple invited me to dine with them. There was a special pilgrims' dinner at a restaurant nearby. It sounded good to me. We walked out of the church and down the street. At the restaurant, the hostess asked us, "Peregrinos?" and we said yes. She led us to a large round table in the back room. She put a menu in front of each of us and asked us if we wanted wine or water. We shared bottles of wine and water. The menu was extensive. I got steak and beef stew with cheese curd for dessert. Cheese curd was like cottage cheese with honey in it. It cost 11 euro each. Everyone got French fries with dinner. I decided to eat there each night while I was in Najera. The second night I went there, the lady recognized me and didn't smile. She didn't take me to the back room with the pilgrims. I had misused my pilgrim status. Pilgrims must move on. The third night I went there, she was openly hostile and wouldn't acknowledge me. A man came and took me to a table. I decided not to go there anymore.

The next day I went to the only market in town that was opened. I found it by asking people on the street, "¿Dónde está un mercado se abra?" It sounded good to me and got results. I saved every bag I got on the Camino. Store clerks really appreciated it when I had my own bag. I folded them up and put them in a baggie in my purse. I used them for laundry, shopping, and trash till they had too many holes in them. At the store, I got chicken and veggies to make a large pot of stew to eat for lunch each day and eggs, veggies, and butter for breakfast. The laundry was in the kitchen but the spin cycle wasn't effective and so I wrapped my clothes in towels to get the water off before hanging them up on the racks also in the kitchen. It was really cold in the hotel. The woman who cleaned each day took pity on me and told the hotel owner to heat the place. Pretty soon, she was there to check it out. Then she sent a repairman to fix it. Yay, heat!

Each evening I went to the church for processions and services. I became a local church lady. It was incredible. I recognized people and they smiled at me. They knew I was a pilgrim though. Boots and shower shoes were all I wore on my feet. My clothes were hiking clothes. Easter was glorious, with drumming and horns and singing. I was surprised and glad to see that new spring clothes on Easter wasn't a Spanish thing and that my pilgrim clothes were just fine.

I worked on my traffic school when I could. The Wi-Fi was good at the hotel. I was surprised that my boots were still wet on Easter, the day before I was to leave. I sloshed in puddles to get the mud off, thinking that my feet wouldn't get wet because the boots were Gore-Tex. Well, my feet were really wet. Hmmm…

I went to a coffee shop. I got myself a cappuccino and a piece of carrot cake to celebrate Easter. I asked if they had any old newspapers. The waitress said no. I explained that I needed to put the newspapers into my boots to dry them. She went in the back and found some for me. I went to the park, sat on the grass, and watched the raging river for a while. I loved how it felt to sit in the park. It was cool and spring-like. I didn't want to do traffic school on Easter, but I felt like I should because the Wi-Fi was so good at the hotel, and I hated to waste it.

CHAPTER 7

VILORIA DE LA RIOJA

226 KM

The day was windy on the open plain and gone were the isolating curving mountain trails. I always felt so lonely walking because I didn't see anyone close to me on the winding trails, except for those passing me. Now that the road was straight and relatively flat, I saw pilgrims in front of and behind me. I bet they had been there all the time but were concealed from me on the mountain trails. That really gave me relief and a better outlook. I got to the place where I had a reservation before noon. They didn't open until 2 pm. I decided to keep going. I tried to contact them to let them know but they weren't answering the phone and they didn't answer the door when I knocked. I was so fit that I needed to walk further each day. I walked on. I called the Refugio Acacio y Orietta Albergue and asked them if I could stay there. The lady said yes but she wouldn't open the door till 2 pm even if it were raining. When I got there, I sat on a bench outside. A couple was waiting across the street and a man was waiting on a rock wall not far off. A skinny mangy-looking cat came over to me and sat next to me. He put his paw on my leg and let one of his claws out to poke me. Ouch! What a weird cat. I ate some lunch from my pack and tried to give scraps of salami to the cat and a little skinny dog who joined us. They strangely didn't want it.

When the door opened, I went in but the lady told me that the couple was there before me. Okay, I stepped back. I had read in a book that crabby people (and maybe cats?) on the Camino were there to cause us to grow. I gave the lady my passport and credential and got my stamp, she told me to leave my boots and poles on the racks by the door. The room came with dinner and breakfast because no restaurant or mercado was open in town. The lady was Orietta. She told us the rules and showed us to the bunk room. There were maybe 4 bunk beds and 4 twin beds. I chose a twin. The couple took a bunk bed. The man took another twin bed. The room was charming with pillars of rough wood holding up the ceiling. A closed fire heater had a sign with a picture of a hand with a red circle and line through it. A sign on one of the pillars outlined meal time, quiet time, and lights out time. Another sign said, "22:00 – 7:00 SILENCIO, RUHE, SILENCE, SILENZIO." My bed looked so inviting. I laid out my sleeping bag, crawled in to get warm and took a nap. I felt really cold. I woke and took a warm shower and brought my laundry to Orietta who was making dinner in the kitchen. I asked her if I could help but she said no. She took my laundry and coins to another room and came back, then asked if I wanted some tea. How nice. The couple was in the living room talking to Acacio in Portuguese. They were from Brazil like Acacio and were enjoying speaking their own language. Orietta was from Italy and had met Acacio on the Camino 13 years before. When he finally talked her into marrying him, they decided to live on the Camino. They ran the albergue because they loved each other, the Camino, and the pilgrims. Acacio was a poet and writer. Orietta showed us a journal on the coffee table for the pilgrims to leave a message. She said that, so far, only women had written in the book. While she was making dinner, she was muttering about how it was difficult to make the right amount of food because a lot of times people make reservations and they don't show up. It was a lot of work for her. I started setting the table. Dinner was divine. The soup was made of zucchini and green beans, smooth and light green, creamy from the blender and warming. We also had salad and pasta, and ice cream bars, or pudding cups for dessert. I kept wanting more soup. The Brazilian couple and I wanted to talk, so Orietta kindly translated for us. I tried to speak some Spanish to them. They encouraged me because they said it was similar to Portuguese. They tried to speak some English to me. We spoke about our children and grandchildren. The single man's name was Paul. He was a retired sewing machine repairman. I told him that I love my sewing machine repairman. He said he still does some repairs for a quilting group in his town of Gualala in northern California. It was a lovely evening and bedtime came too soon.

In the morning, we had toast, eggs, coffee, and yogurt for breakfast. We were all hustling to get out of there on time. When we were packing up, Paul told me that his knee was giving him pain. I told him about tying a bandana around the patella below the knee. He thanked me, then he looked sad and said, "But my bandana is packed already." Before I left, I made an entry in the journal on the coffee table. It was a picture of the straight trail leading up to mountains of green with a blue sky above and a pilgrim waving and saying Thank You.

At the door, I put on my rain poncho. I hoisted my pack on like usual and Orietta stopped me and told me to put it down. She untightened my straps all the way and told me to put it on. Then she tightened my waist strap and the side straps and then the chest strap and then the side ones again. She said if I put it on without loosening the straps, I would hurt my shoulders. Wow, I learned something new and useful.

It was lovely that she took the time to show me the right way. We left in whipping wind and rain.

Too soon, and before we got to a town, I had to wee. I was walking on a wide trail right next to the freeway where many trucks were passing. I looked for a wall or a tree, but there was none. There were short pillars along the way. I felt really sad that I didn't have a skirt so I could just lower my knickers and not have to bare my butt. Then I realized that my poncho was like a skirt. So, I leaned up against a pillar with my back to the freeway, positioned my poncho around me, I pulled 'em down and commenced. Just then a wind came up and made my poncho airborne. I tried to pull it down around me again. A trucker honked in appreciation. So, I unceremoniously put myself together and thought, *Well, I will never see these people again*. Ugh… I vowed to get a longer poncho with arms in it like some other pilgrims had. It wouldn't blow over my head as easily. One trouble with peeing on the fly was that I had so many pieces of clothing on: tights, undershirt, shirt, money belt, pants, and jacket all had to be dealt with every time. Not to mention the bag and backpack and poles and gloves. It was quite an operation. I also decided that three cups of coffee in the morning isn't a good idea if the next bar wasn't close.

The rain turned to sleet. In the afternoon we had rainbows. I loved the weather. Flowers seemed appreciative of the rain. They were everywhere, waving in the wind. Low bushes of pink flowers danced and fields of bushes with silver fuzzy pods rippled and stood strong. Bright red poppies seemed to be dancing in the wind. An area of twiggy trees growing close to each other had sky and mountains showing through. They filled the horizon and seemed to go on forever. Breathing, foot beats, and pole cadence kept me steady uphill and down. Over the top of a hill, I viewed a beautiful green field under grey and white cumulus clouds, a bridge over a river, and a forest in the distance. Muddy puddles were everywhere. It was 37 degrees Fahrenheit that morning when I left. An hour later it was 36. Burr! The afternoon proved to be 62 degrees, which was pleasant for hiking.

CHAPTER 8

THE ENGLISH GUY AT THE MONASTERY

260 KM

I walked through two little towns and then up a tall hill and into a forest. I met up with the woman from the Albergue de Abuelita in Los Arcos who had hurting knees. I noticed she had bandanas tied on each of her legs below her knees. She thanked me for telling her about the bandanas because she could walk and didn't have to go home. That made me happy.

The last leg of the walk was 12 km. That's 17 km for the day. I got lost a couple of times. My Camino app sorted it out. I think some degenerates were painting yellow arrows in the wrong places. So, Yay for my app. This part of the Camino had a bunch of alternative routes. I felt like I was way out in left field, but my app said I was on the Camino. I walked by a giant space-age-looking military base. Two guys passed me but they were the only people I saw all day. I left the bushes behind a while back. Only barren rocky dirt could be seen everywhere with some scruffy grass here and there. I could see a town far off in the distance, not sure if the trail went that way. I was all alone so I tried the SheWee. It was confusing to know which was the front and which was the back. I unzipped and held it in place. A lot went out of the spout but not all. So, I tied a jacket around my waist and hoped my pants would be dry before I got to a town. Whateverrrrrrr. I was so glad to see San Roque. I stayed at a monastery with 60 bunk beds. I got the last lower bunk in the second bunk room. I took a shower and went down to wash my clothes with ice water in the cement laundry sink in the garden. No centrifuge, so my socks would be 3 days drying. Communal dinner was at 6:30 pm. I heard they were famous for the garlic soup for peregrinos.

Dinner was in a big dining hall with many room-long tables and chairs. The dinner line began with a tray; one lady put a bowl of soup on my tray, the next young man served a bowl of spaghetti, and then we were to pick up a bowl of salad from a table where they were laid out for us and a little cup of watered-down fruit juice. I also saw a bowl of dinner rolls and a larger bowl of fruit. I was so hungry, I felt like eating everything in sight. A young woman told us to take just one.

I didn't know where to sit. I spied an empty seat and brought my tray to almost the end of a table by the wall and sat down. Across the table and to the right a young man from England and a middle-aged lady from the United States sat together. Also, a man sat next to me. A couple sat down across from me but they moved before I got to know them. Then a happy, scruffy monk-looking pilgrim sat down. The English guy asked me why I decided to walk the Camino. I told him about my husband who had died after a long illness and my mother who died a few months later. I had cared for my husband who had Parkinson's Disease for 17 years and he was totally disabled from

2010 to 2018 when he died. My girlfriend walked the Camino and I yearned to go too. I decided that when I was done with caregiving, I would go to Spain and walk the Camino. He said that was a lot to take care of him for so long. I told him that we were in a support group and one of the women told me that she hadn't signed up for this caregiving gig. I told her that I did. In our wedding ceremony, when I repeated "in sickness and in health, till death do us part," I took it very seriously. I was 20 years old, and I remembered thinking that my life wasn't my own any more. I was committed to being Ron's wife whatever happened. I told him that our lives hadn't been all roses. We both had rough childhoods and had buttons that got pushed a lot through the years. We had five children and were involved in our church, so we had many distractions and a lot of reasons and support for staying together.

I asked him why he was walking the Camino. He was in the military and had just had a short time to be on the Camino. He had to leave and go back in a couple of days. The lady next to him nudged him and told him to tell me the rest. He looked uncomfortable and told me that he had married, his wife had a child, and he had left her. He realized he had gotten married too young. He was there to sort things out and hopefully find himself. I told him I was sorry. He looked sheepish and said yeah. The lady next to him gave a little smile of approval.

I told him that one thing to think about was that if his wife found someone else, no one she could ever find was going to love his child as much as he did. He said, yeah. I told him about Ho'oponopono, a healing technique for families, how it cleans relationships; and that it's like magic. We all have people in our lives who make us unhappy. We need to cut the binds of discontent that we have with people. If we loosen these binds, we can have a more peaceful relationship with them afterwards. It's all about clearing what's in us that attracts sad experiences. We all want to be happy. We have buttons that get pushed that bring us back to our trauma from the past that can be released. I wrote the Ho'oponopono down on a paper so he could take it with him. His friend took a picture of it with her phone so she could have it too.

It seemed like divine providence that I sat across from him. I had a mental picture of our guardian angels pushing us in all the right directions to get us there like that.

The guy across from me was from Spain. He said he was studying to become a religious monk and he was on the Camino as part of his formation. The guy next to me was from Holland. He said he had finished a job and was going to have a new job in a couple of weeks, so he took this in-between time to be on the Camino.

The server came around with the spaghetti pot asking if anyone wanted some more. I raised my hand. After I stowed my dishes and silverware, I went up to my bunk, got ready for bed, and went to dreamland till the snoring got rough. Ugh.

In the morning, I got my stuff together, I pinned my two pairs of socks onto my pack to let them dry as I walked. There was no breakfast. I went down to the entrance put on my boots and grabbed my poles. I saw the young Englishman. He smiled at me and said that he wouldn't forget what I said and that I had a big effect on him. I tried to tell him something more about Ho'oponopono, but he stopped me and said that I had already changed his life and that was enough.

Outside, next door to the monastery, was a restaurant. The owner was out front and told me that he wasn't open yet. Oh well, there was another town not far away. When I asked him where the Camino was, he pointed. My boots crunched across the decomposed granite parking lot and, finding an arrow, I walked down the right road.

CHAPTER 9

BURGOS

285 KM

The night before I left for Burgos, one of the men at my albergue told me that after Villafria, it was a 9-km walk on the freeway to Burgos. He was going to take an alternate route through a park, but I was thinking that there would be no arrows, and I didn't want to get lost. He encouraged me to walk through the park; it was longer but not on the freeway. I asked him if he would walk slowly with me and he looked at me and said nothing. I told him I didn't want to be out in the park alone and get lost.

The next day, I walked 18 K to Villa Fria and took the bus to Burgos from there. I really wanted to walk the whole way, but not 9 km on the freeway. I decided that taking the bus was part of the Camino experience. It was better to not have a perfect Camino. The imperfections would make this experience my own.

I met a woman at a bar that morning. She was at a table with another woman and I asked if I could sit with them. She was quite reserved and her friend was colorful and boisterous; we chatted and laughed together. I got on the road and left them there. Later in the day, when I got to Villafria, I went into a bar to ask where to take the bus. That same reserved woman was in the bar. We were surprised to see each other. She said she remembered me because of my green earrings and that she didn't think I would make it that far that day. Well, I made it that far but I was going to take the bus the rest of the way to Burgos. I waited for the bus and then I waited for the bus driver to eat his dinner. I gave the driver his fare and told him to tell me when we got to Burgos. It was quite a way off the freeway through many towns of varying sizes.

The bus filled up with riders and then emptied several times. It was almost dark when I got to Burgos.

The bus driver let me off in the heart of town. I showed people on the street the address of my hotel. One man told me where to go. When I got there, it was the wrong place. Then another man told me he would take me there. I followed him in the opposite direction. I was so happy when it was the right place. He rang the bell and made sure it was the place where I had a reservation. He was my angel in disguise. The woman in charge took my money for three nights. My friends from Valcarlos told me, on our WhatsApp, that I should stay longer in Burgos to see the cathedral and the museum. Also, I needed to complete my traffic school. I was so glad to see they had an elevator. My room was nice. It had two twin beds, one to throw my stuff on and one to sleep in. It also had a large wooden armoire. A small sink was in the corner and the bathroom with a large bathtub was down the hall. I purchased some bath-soak at the mercado the next day. Since I kept my pack very light, I had to buy a new bottle of bath-soak every time I got to a bathtub. The mercado had some bath-soak with Epsom salts that was divine. There was no kitchen in the hotel so I would have to eat out or have food that didn't need cooking. I ate food from my backpack that night. I felt like I had walked enough that day, about 18 K, so I went to bed early.

I slept through the night. I woke up at 11:11am, a great sign of divinity. I got my clothes together to go to the laundromat. I walked around looking for a laundromat. I was telling God that it was alright to help me find one. I asked some other peregrinos if they had found one. They said no. Then some ladies came to me and were talking to me in Spanish. I thought they were asking me for help. Then I realized that they wanted to help me. I said, "Quiero lavar mi ropa." They looked at each other and said "ropa" together. The younger woman left the older woman standing there and took me two blocks over and showed me the laundromat. She went in to make sure it was open. Wow! When I sat down and looked at my phone it was 1:11 pm. Okay, Thank You, God. A laundromat I had used in another town had soap in the machine already. I tried to ask the lady in the chair next to me if I needed to put soap in the machine. I couldn't remember the word for soap. We went back and forth a while and she didn't understand my question. Then I looked up soap on my phone translator. Jabón, "¿Hay jabón in la máquina?" She said, "Si, no agregue jabón extra." For some reason, I kept getting confused about which was the washer and which was the dryer. I paid for what I thought was the washer but it was the dryer, so I paid for the washer and by the time the washer was done, the dryer had timed out and I had to pay again. It seemed fine to me. I was just trying and failing and trying again. I was fine with my learning curve. I took my clothes back to my room and hung up the -ion clothes that didn't go into the dryer. Then, I went out to find food.

I found a coffee shop that had delicious pictures of food. I went in and sat at the counter. I told the very handsome young guy "café con leche." and grabbed a menu and pointed to a meat and tomato dish. He brought me the thinly cut ham on crostini with no tomatoes. I pointed to the tomatoes in the picture and asked "¿Dónde están los tomates?" He looked at me and told someone else to get tomatoes. They didn't. Then when he came back, I asked, "¿Tomates?" He brought me a few pieces but not as many as in the picture.

My phone card was out of service and I needed to get another one. I got to Burgos Friday evening and the lady at the hotel said the phone store wouldn't be open till Monday morning. She recommended I try to get a phone card at the grocery store. The lady at the store said they used to have phone cards but not anymore. She said to go to a newspaper kiosk. The lady at the kiosk told me I would have to have a phone number first. My phone number was British so that wouldn't work. I walked all over town looking for a phone card and I got lost. My feet were hurting from so much action in my shower shoes without my orthotic. My boots were still wet. Google maps got me back to the hotel. I was surprised that google maps was working with a used-up sim.

A gelato shop was right down the street from my hotel. It was in front of a snack market that had dried fruit, candy, and nuts. I got some raisins and nuts and decided that gelato and raisins and nuts was probably a good meal. On the way back to my hotel, I saw a beer garden with tablesful of talking, laughing people outside. I wanted to get a beer and join in the fun; but I thought, *No, I must take my traffic school test, and I would not be able to do that successfully if I had a cerveza. I would just fall asleep or do badly on the test.* I went up to my room and sat on my bed and took the test. The internet was fast and made it easy but it took a long time. I was really careful and read things more than once. I didn't want to have to take it again. I passed! Yay! The beer garden was closed by the time I finished my test. So, I had nuts and raisins for dinner, took a quick shower, and went to bed.

There were so many choices for churches to go to Mass on Sunday. I had an app on my phone that found area churches and gave Mass times! Several large beautiful cathedral-like churches were within walking distance. I chose the one near the canal, St. Lesmes Abad, because it was the closest and had Mass at 11 am. I loved being in the old church, sitting with the people and it was easy to spot the other pilgrims because they had hiking boots and attire on. Some hikers even came in with their packs on, fresh off the Camino, dirt, mud, and all. I loved seeing them. After Mass, they had a pilgrim blessing. The priest brought us up to the front, blessed us for our journey, and asked God to keep us safe so we could all make it home safely to our families at the end of our Camino.

Walking down to the river near where the bus driver left me off, I looked for a place to eat. I saw a hamburger/pizza restaurant. I was interested to find out what the Spanish did with a hamburger. I had to wait for a table. I ended up sitting near the food prep station. I was impressed at the freshness of the food. The servers put together beautiful salads and layered tomatoes, red onion slices, and lettuce on the hamburgers from bins of fresh vegetables. The pizzas had really fresh mushrooms and peppers and onions. I got a hamburger and a coke. It was delicious. I never drink coke, but it just seemed right. After dinner, I took a peaceful stroll along the river's grassy edge. I found a park with shade trees, benches, statues, and fountains. A family with children and parents were playing with a ball in their Sunday-best clothes. I walked up a street around some homes and enjoyed the sweet smell of the flower gardens under the deep shade of trees. The homes were stately and of old grey stone. I saw a giant portico and entered it. I was immediately in another world. It was bustling with cars, buses, a lot of families out walking, and toy stores and gift shops were open. I spied the Vodaphone store that the hotel lady told me about. I would have to go there in the morning before I left town.

Monday morning, I got all packed up, put on my still damp boots, grabbed my poles, and walked down the street toward the Vodaphone store. I stopped in at a bar for breakfast. The proprietor was a large man behind the bar. I ordered the biggest breakfast on the menu with beef and eggs and a café con leche. I felt like I needed some strengthening food. He told me to sit at a dining table and he would serve me there. There was a friendly man at the bar sipping on something amber in a short glass. He seemed delighted that I was there. Some people are just plain doting on pilgrims. I had a duffel bag that I had acquired on a previous day. I asked him if I could give it to him so I wouldn't have to carry it. He said he had a use for it. Great!

When I got to the Vodaphone store, one of the sales reps called me over. I was so happy that I could have phone service for a month for 30 euros. She set it up, put the sim in my phone, and wanted to give me a bunch of paperwork that I wasn't willing to carry on the Camino. So, I gave it back to her. She put together the things I needed and taped them onto the little envelope that held my old sim. I almost left my poles when I exited the store but I went back and grabbed them. I used my Mass finder to find the cathedral and the museum.

The cathedral was a tourist destination. I walked up the many stairs out front and found that I would have to stow my backpack in the museum's basement. So, I went down again and down the block and around the corner to find the museum lower entrance. The lady in the basement gave me a key and told me to put my pack in the locker through the turn-style which I did. I went back up the stairs. I paid the pilgrim's fee and got an audio speaker to tell me all about it. I spent all day in the cathedral and the museum. The cathedral was resplendent with stained glass windows, dark wood altar, and choir lofts. Alcoves all around the perimeter had altars dedicated to different stories of the life of Christ and the saints. A statue of pregnant Mary, the mother of God was unique. One had a recognizably ancient stocky wooden statue of

Mary sitting holding Jesus similar to those I'd seen in the other churches of Spain. One area of the cathedral had a ceiling that looked like looking up into heaven. The audio said it was the first of its kind in antiquity. It was a bunch of star windows up high in a dome shape that let light in, and it glowed bright and heavenly. Other memorable items were the statues of happy princes and princesses of a certain era. They were beautifully life-like and carved out of wood painted delicately. Their beauty took my breath away. I saw the coffin of El Cid. It was exciting for me to see because a statue of El Cid on a horse stands in Balboa Park in my hometown of San Diego, which is full of Spanish architecture. One Spanish dignitary said that Balboa Park was more Spanish than Spain! The museum was full of paintings, model buildings in many glowing colors, and architectural drawings by Gaudi.

I stayed probably longer than I should have. Finally, I got on the road and started looking for arrows. Down by the river I asked a woman where the Camino was. She started to point up a hill away from the river and then said, "No, I have to go that way anyway. Follow me." So, we walked along the river and talked. I told her she was my angel that God sent to lead me out of Burgos. She was pleased and said that if that were all she had to do to be an angel, she was glad. She said she believed in angels too. She was happy to practice speaking English to a native English speaker. She was an English teacher there in Burgos. She told me about her life. She was a single woman and was stressed with so many things to do and cope with. I told her about my miracle prayer, "Dear God, please make everything turn out okay.' Then you let God make everything turn out okay. God is good at it and really likes us to acknowledge it. Miracles happen when I say that prayer." She said she would try it. We came to a bridge across the river. She said to go across the bridge and I would find the yellow arrows of the Camino.

CHAPTER 10

SAN BOL

312 KM

Hiking - I don't like either the word or
The thing. People ought to saunter in
The mountains - not hike! Do you know
The origin of that word 'saunter?' It's a
Beautiful word. Away back in the
Middle Ages people used to go on
Pilgrimages to the Holy Land, and
When people in the villages through
Which they passed asked where they

*Were going, they would reply, "A la
sainte terre,' 'To the Holy Land.' And
So they became as
Sainte-Terre-ers or saunterers. Now
These mountains are our Holy Land,
And we ought to saunter through them
Reverently, not 'hike' through them.*
—*John Muir*

I love this quote by John Muir. I remember my grandmother on my mother's side. I used to say she strolled
when she walked. She walked with a soft heel strike and
took her time. I supposed she sauntered. The usual time
recommended to walk the Camino was 30 to 35 days. I
sauntered the Camino in 66 days. I took most weekends,
a few sick days, and, Holy Week off too. I had a problem
with my foot, pes cavus, caused by high arches. I wore
an orthotic in my shoes. I did Tai Chi walking for relief
on the Camino: rolling my foot and lifting it completely off the ground at the end of each step really helped
reduce the pain. I kept going. I wore negative ion socks
that infused negative ions (which are very health and
comfort giving) into my feet as I sauntered.

Walking the Meseta was wonderful. People told me that it would be boring. That was so untrue. The farms on the Meseta create an interesting and lush landscape. There were small barren areas, so you could see what the Meseta was about. Because of modern farming techniques, it was a lush area with green and sometimes flowered crops growing as far as you could see. I would choose walking the Meseta over walking up hills any day.

One evening, while walking the Meseta, I came to San Bol. It was way out of the way. Nothing was near. It was a strange building that was obviously very old. The building had a giant shell painted on the presenting wall and a giant egg dome out the top to one side. My guide book recommended it as a good place to stay. I was tired when I got there, so I went in and selected a bed. No one seemed to be in charge. A few pilgrims were sitting outside. Rosa arrived a little later, took our euros, and stamped our credentials. She recommended that we buy dinner because there was no place to eat close by. There was a locked cupboard with snacks we could purchase. I got a tube of digestive biscuits. Rosa came each day to cook dinner and check people in. She went into the kitchen to make dinner, while the whole albergue filled up. The 6 bunk beds were all full by dinner time. They had an upstairs, but it was closed. They would need the extra room later in the summer.

The story goes that you won't have problems with your feet if you soak them in the pool at the bottom of the garden. I walked down to the pool beneath the trees. It was deep, and you couldn't see the bottom for the algae. I sat on the cement ledge surrounding the pool and put my feet in. It was so cold it was numbing and when I wasn't watching, green algae wrapped itself around my feet. My feet felt good about an hour later when I could finally feel them again. People who were passing by and not staying at San Bol came to soak their feet too. I grabbed a tub from up at the patio and took it down to the pool to wash my clothes. There was an outlet at the lower edge of the pool. It must have been an artesian well, as the water kept spilling out, creating an area of lush vegetation below. I hung my clothes on the patio clothesline. It was almost full but I found some space.

In the dining room, a giant wooden round table

with 12 chairs filled the dome room. We would be pilgrims of the round table at dinner. As 6 o'clock drew near, the smell of the paella drew us all together. Our paella was rice, seafood, chicken, and vegetables cooked in a giant round shallow pan. We also shared a big bowl of salad, and flan was our dessert. What a totally Spanish dinner! Two young men and a young woman were there. One man and the woman were friendly and participated in the conversation; the other younger man obviously didn't want to be there. He scowled and looked down most of the time. Wow, the dynamics were heady. The older young man seemed to be patient and to be lovingly caring for the younger one. We were a good mix of women and men. There was a hippy-looking group with really fun loose cotton clothing with natural touches like feathers and sheepskin, a single man, and two other young women. I enjoyed the conversation at dinner. A mascot graced one of the walls of the dining room. It was a pilgrim effigy and was the subject of our amusement.

I took a late shower after dinner and went to bed, hoping to get some sleep before the snoring started. Breakfast was a bunch of packaged food Rosa left out for us. Granola bars, cookies, and trail mix packets and yogurt in the fridge. She left the coffee ready to be plugged in. Some pilgrims left early but some of us were there for breakfast. Rather than carry my digestive biscuits with me, I gave them to the hippies.

I hated to leave; it was such a charming place. I packed up and went out into the cool, crisp morning. I could feel the freshness all around and after practically gliding up the hill, I was on with my day of walking through the countryside to Santiago. Fields stretched out as far as the eye could see, some with plants and some with acres of tan cloddy dirt, waiting to be planted. I came to a grass and rock trail with stone walls on each side. A town became visible in the distance, and my first thought was, *Good, I have to go.* Red poppies smiled and danced in the wind on each side. Little bushes along with giant windmills accentuated the blue sky across a field. Down the middle of the road that went through the town was a strip of stone bricks, a shell design placed every few feet. I loved the way the towns created their own special displays of their dedication to the Camino, like gifts to make us feel at home.

I'll never forget Ruinas del Convento de San Antón (Siglo XV). Walking on the trail through fields, I came over a small hill and saw ruins in the distance. It looked magical, with gigantic arches and spires with pointed cupolas. As I walked closer, I could see that it was a stunning ruin of rare beauty. Someone in antiquity had an idea to make this beautiful convent way out here, probably just for the glory of God. As I walked through the gaping arches, Irish fairy harp music filled the air. A concession was set up under an arch to the side. A Filipino man with a plaid kilt about his loins and wearing a white t-shirt was behind the counter, making egg salad sandwiches, shoving them into sandwich bags, and stacking them up next to juice bottles in a refrigerated display case. A pot of coffee groaned away on the counter. He also had a watermelon ready to cut up in case anyone wanted some. I asked him where the restroom was. He pointed to a distant trailer. I was there in a flash, I opened the door and stepped inside. Then I realized how rickety it was. The closed door didn't really conceal completely, close enough though. I appreciated the opportunity to sit down and wee in peace. I got a cup of cafe con leche from the concession and sat at a table enjoying it. As I walked on, the delightful magical feeling in my heart was lovely.

About the time I had to wee again, I arrived at St. Nicholas Chapel. The Knights Templars had been stationed there and were said to still be there to watch over the peregrinos. The dimly lit room was gigantic and occupied the whole building except for a loft above to one side. Short black capes were hanging on the walls around the room with white shells and red dagger crosses appliqued on them. An altar at the far end of the room had a rope around it, emphasizing the sacredness of the sanctuary. It was also an albergue. The bunks were upstairs in the loft. The building had no electricity but the restroom trailer out back did. When I walked in, a woman with a metal pitcher of warm café con leche was pouring small cups for the pilgrims. She would leave and refill her pitcher when she ran out. The little cups were plastic. I noticed that she rinsed them out with water in between servings. Improvising on the Camino, she had such a big heart and wanted something nice for each of us. She was just a little shady on the dishwashing routine.

One thing I noticed along the way were many white horses in fields. I imagined that they were the ancestors of the horses ridden by the Knights Templars.

CHAPTER II

THE GUY AT SAHAGÚN

410 KM

I pretty much walked alone all day. My breath was visible in the morning but it was 62 degrees F by the afternoon. Sometimes it felt hot while I was walking, then a cool breeze wafted and I was glad I hadn't taken my jacket off. I spent my walking solitude designing in my head how I would make a skirt out of my pair of yoga pants so I could pee without exposing my backside. I kept seeing the same people again and again during the day, since I wasn't walking so slowly anymore. I felt like the Energizer Bunny after I asked God to put a skip in my step.

I came across amazing bodegas tunneled into the hillsides complete with doors and entryways. Some were like houses built into the hill. I read a sign that said Las Bodegas de Moratinos. It read they belonged to families and they were dug by the children during the winter months. One hill had a bunch of entrances and at the top of the hill was a chimney and a TV antenna.

Further along, I saw a large town in the far distance to the left. The yellow arrow on the trail turned off to the right though. The topography was flat with scrubby grasslands and a few trees and bushes. It was stunningly beautiful. I could see far away to the horizon. After a long peaceful saunter, the trail led to a stone church that was closed. In a field to the left was a huge portal with giant, larger-than-life-sized carved stone statues of a man and a woman and a friar in medieval attire. The trail led up to the portal so I had to step over a large stone that had Camino de Santiago carved into it. Then the trail led back to the town.

I walked into Sahagún, the halfway mark on the

Camino Frances. I was thinking that the portal may have been the halfway mark. I didn't know. Sahagún was a large town with suburbs. The outer neighborhoods made walking into town one anticlimax after another as I kept not getting there. Finally, I was in the town center. There was almost no one on the streets. I asked the few people I saw for directions along the way, showing them the address of the monastery in my guide book. I asked everyone I saw, refining my search with each request. Finally, I was on the right street. All the manhole covers had the beautiful Sahagún logo with a coat of arm. It seemed to be a proud town. I passed a closed hardware store that had a sewing thread display in the window, thinking I would return later. When I got to the monastery, the door was locked. A man came to unlock it and ushered me in. He showed me to a chair near the cheerful monk who was sitting at a desk with a bowl of wrapped fruity candy next to him. He was signing people in. When it was my turn, I gave him my passport and credential. He wrote everything down, gave me my stamp and handed them back to me. It was 12 euros for the bed. Dinner would be after Mass. They were going to keep us busy: Sharing was at 5, Mass at 6:30, Blessing at 7, potluck at 8, bed by 10 pm, up at 7:15 am, breakfast at 7:40, out by 8:30.

He took me to a small room with two bunk beds and a large window that looked out at the garden. Stuff was on all the beds, so I didn't know which to take. He told me to take any bunk I wanted. He said that the group that was there had stayed too long and had taken over the place. I needed to stake my claim. I moved the stuff off one of the bottom bunks. I laid down to take a nap.

When I woke, the others had gotten back, there was Liam from Ireland and Greg from the UK and Inga from Germany. I asked if anyone wanted to do laundry. They said yes. We got our clothes together and went to the laundry room. We all put our clothes in the machine, I gave my coin and we left the clothes washing. I went back to the room to take a shower and then went out to the garden courtyard in the middle of the monastery where they were all sitting at a table sharing a salad that Carol from Napa Valley and Karen from Australia made. They insisted that I eat with them. They had an extra fork and someone gave me their plate. The salad was beautiful with lettuce, olives, tomatoes, and pomegranate, cheese, pumpkin seeds, and tangy salad dressing. I was surprised when Liam said that he had already hung up the laundry. He pointed up to the second story balcony that surrounded the whole patio. There were racks with lots of people's clothes. He smiled sheepishly and admitted that he felt a thrill when he hung up my bra.

I asked him why he had come to the Camino. He told his story. He had lived with his two brothers in the family house after his parents moved to Dublin. His older brother left to get a job in another town. He stayed till the younger brother graduated from high school. Now Liam wanted to leave too but the younger brother got angry and didn't want him to. He had guilt feelings about leaving but he needed to leave. He hoped to get some clarity on the Camino.

I spoke up and told him to imagine a best-case scenario. I told him to make up the best story he could think of for his brother. "When you worry about him, it's like making up a bad story and having faith in the bad outcome. You can change things up with your thoughts. What we say, we name. What we name we make real. Besides, it will make you happy to make up a good story. It's best to make yourself happy for now. Then you can attract more good things with your good vibrations. It doesn't matter what happened before. What you think now creates your future. Entertaining thoughts about what happened before brings in the future on that track, so if you want the future to be different, you have to think differently. Make up a story about how you want it to be and that will pull what you want forward. It has a lot to do with vibration. Discontent has a low vibration so if you think about the discontent, the vibration you send out pulls in more discontent."

Liam looked at me with skepticism.

"How do you want your brother to feel?" I asked.

"I want him to be happy." Liam answered

"What would make him happy?"

"Living with family would make him happy."

"How can you make that happen? Imagine him happy, what else is going on?"

"Our whole family is together."

"So, what else can you think of that would be close to that and happy?"

"Well, if I take away my older brother and myself, my parents are left. I had thought of taking him to live with my parents. I may just do that. My brother is their responsibility, not mine." He looked relieved.

After lunch, they invited me to walk with them to the museum to get our halfway certificate. I asked them about dinner. They said there would be a communal dinner with shared dishes that everyone would contribute. We could stop at the supermercado on the way back to get food. I was thrilled that they let me into their group and they wanted to take me along with them. After quite a trek, we got to the museum. It was a modern building with walls of windows. Inside was a clerk at a desk behind a window. She took our money and checked our passports and credentials. Then we all went to explore the museum. There were floors of giant exhibits of meaningful stark and simple colorful art. Some areas looked ancient. They must have built the large building around the ancient building or somehow moved an ancient building's interior. There was a choir room paneled in beautiful old carved wood with fold-down choir chairs built into the walls. Liam came into the room and made a loud tone with his voice and laughed. I was surprised. He was obviously enjoying himself. Carol shushed him. We went downstairs through a photo exhibit of immigrants from many African and Middle Eastern countries. Our certificates were ready and we picked them up. I got a tube for mine. Then I realized that I was trying to not carry anything extra and now I would be carrying this thing.

We went to the grocery store. I got a large round loaf of bread, yogurt, frozen spinach, sliced salami, and lettuce. They asked me if I knew how to get back to the monastery and I said, "No." So, they waited for me.

When we got back to the monastery where the monks were starting the discussion groups. My friends explained that they had been to the monastery discussions and dinner on a previous night and they were going out for dinner. The doorman cautioned them to get back before 10 pm or they would be locked out. I stayed and participated in the discussions. The monks made sure we each had a cup of tea and a snack. The groups were separated according to the languages spoken. The English group was led by the monk who signed us in. He explained that he was the only one who spoke a little English and he apologized and said that he would do his best but he didn't speak English perfectly. We all shared what brought us to the Camino, then any problem we were willing to share about our spiritual path.

After the group, I went to the kitchen to prepare the food I bought to share. I found some serving dishes and washed the lettuce and made lettuce wraps with the sausage. Someone found some toothpicks to hold them together. Then I pulled the middle out of the bread and mixed the yogurt with the spinach and some vegetable soup powder and filled the bread bowl with it. I put it in the fridge and rushed off to the pilgrims' Mass in the chapel. I was late.

At the service, in an ancient and beautiful chapel, eight monks were on one side of the altar and six sisters were on the other. All the pews were filled with pilgrims. After Mass, two of the sisters came forward and invited the pilgrims to stand up front. One of the nuns handed us each a colorful paper with a blessing on it, each in their own language. The head of the monastery stood up and read the blessing in Spanish and blessed each of us. And the nun put her hands on our shoulders with a loving smile. They were blessing us for our pilgrimage.

Back at the monastery, I got my food out of the fridge and balancing both dishes, I brought them down the hall to the dining room. On the way, the dish with the lettuce wraps tipped and many were on the floor. A smiling monk told me to keep going and he would take care of it. There was so much love there. Nothing went wrong even when it did. In the dining hall was a giant table made up of many tables lined up about 30 feet long. The food was all along the middle of the table. There wasn't an empty chair. A monk got up and gave me his seat. I tried to refuse but he said the dinner was for the pilgrims. I sat across from two smiling men from the Philippines. I met a fit elderly couple from France who had been walking the Camino for five years constantly, and they traveled many other trails and pilgrimages in that time too. We shared the dishes and periodically one of the monks would bring dishes from other parts of the table and the food was traded around. We listened to the English-speaking monk share about the history of the monastery and the need for volunteers. We could all be volunteers when we came back to the Camino next time. He shared about his order and their world-wide outreach. We were invited to stay and talk and come for breakfast between 6:00 and 8:00 in the morning. We were all expected to be on our way by 8:30 am.

I got back to the room and stowed my gear ready for my quick retreat in the morning. I put my sleep sack nighty on, put in my earplugs, and pulled down my stocking cap over eyes, and drifted off to sleep. The others came in after 11:00 pm! I asked them how they got in. The Irish guy with his charming smile said he had an agreement with the doting doorkeeper.

In the morning, I got dressed, grabbed my pack, and went to the dining hall. There was bread and a couple of toasters and jars of different nut butters and bowls of fruit. I noticed three flavors of Nutella hiding in the back behind the other nut butters, yum.

We left together like the five musketeers on the adventure of our lives. We spotted a bar in one of the towns but Liam said "I never stop at the first bar." We returned, finding no other bar in the town. They had large round tables. Liam bought a jug of wine and olives and crusty bread and oil with balsamic vinegar and cups all around. I tried to give him some money and he said that I could get it another time. This is how they did it.

We marched on two by three, sharing stories and jokes, changing partners, and having a good time. We walked past farms and fields, and gardens, up-hill and down over bridges over rivers with wavy green slime and ferns. We trudged over a dry area with the gravel crunching under our boots, sandals, and sneakers. The wind whipped up and slowed us down.

Inga told me she had a room at a pension in Calzadilla de Los Hermanillos. A room with a bathtub! Wow, I wasn't thinking of staying in a private room; but a tub sounded wonderful. I called ahead and was told that they had a room without a tub available. I told her I didn't think so. Then she said she could give me a room with a tub because a lady hadn't arrived yet. I stopped at a small market while the others went on ahead. It was closed, but when the proprietor saw me, he came out and opened the door. I got some bath soak along with some food for the next day.

Following the arrows and in the high wind now,

I arrived. The hotel looked like a house from the outside with an iron gate, flowering vines on the stone walls, and a stone-paved walkway and porch. When I got inside, a reception area led into a giant dining room and a wide welcoming stairway went up to the rooms. The lady pointed to the large container for hiking sticks where I deposited mine. I got worried and told the lady that I didn't want to take the room from my friends who also wanted a bathtub. She said not to worry about it. I got the room and dinner and breakfast. The internet was down so they wanted me to pay with my card in the morning before I left. I asked her if there were any church services. She said the ladies of the town said the rosary at 5 pm in the church in the middle of town.

The room at the top of the stairs was nice and basic. There was a double bed with a white chenille bedspread, a nightstand with a small lamp, a chair, and a desk by the window that looked out on lovely dark green trees. I was glad to see an extra electrical receptacle for my phone. The tub was calling to me, so I started the water and added the bath soak. The bath was warming on a cold, windy day. I rested in the warm water until it was time to get dressed to go out to the church.

When I got to the small plain stone church in the middle of town, I walked all the way around it. There was a crowd of older ladies in coats or jackets near one of the doors. They were waiting. Ten minutes later, a woman came and took a key out of her pocket and opened the door. We all shuffled in and knelt down. Someone started the rosary. It pleased me to be there praying with them. The church was simple inside and out.

At dinner, I sat across from a lady and her teenage daughter. They said they were really enjoying their time together. They were with several women who were with a tour group that made reservations at hotels for them. One of the women said she had the handicapped room downstairs like usual because she walked slowly and the rooms with tubs were gone when she got there. Oh my, so this was the person who was supposed to have my room. The proprietor gave us a menu. When I ordered the fish soup he smiled broadly. When he brought the soup, it had a large shrimp with jutting eyeballs in the middle of it. I tried to eat the shrimp, but it was obviously a decoration. It was too stiff to take apart. The dinner was delicious. When the chef brought the desert, he was excited to give it to us and said it was special local honey with special local cheese slices. It was on a little plate that we shared between us all. This is where I learned to love the local soft sharp cheese.

CHAPTER 12

MOTHER'S DAY

454 KM

A young man from Poland came to me one evening asking for advice for dealing with his flu symptoms. As I backed away, I offered him a bouillon cube. He said he had some and thanked me for the good idea. Oh man, I guess I seemed like a mother or grandmother figure to him. All I could think of was I don't want to get sick. I didn't want his germs.

That night there was a snoring chorus that was too much for my ear plugs. I was glad to be awake though to do breathing exercises because I was feeling warnings of a stuffy nose and phlegm in my throat. In the morning, Miranda, who was snoring loudly, exclaimed that the snoring was loud that night. I guessed it was loud for her until she fell asleep and joined the chorus.

On the trail, I met a lady named Geraldine. She was from New York. First, I passed her, which was a novel experience because people usually passed me. I never passed people up. We passed each other up most of the day. I stopped into a bar to get cafe con leche and use the facilities. I asked her if she wanted to come with me. She said no, she had to keep walking or she would never get there. I sauntered into the patio of the bar and noticed some ladies I had seen before. They were drinking what looked like beer. One lady told me it was beer with lemon. She said it was very refreshing. I ordered one. I watched the bartender pour half a glass of beer from the tap, and then he took out a chilled 2-liter bottle of lemon soda and filled the rest of the glass. My friend was right. It was amazingly refreshing. One of the ladies in the group had on a voluminous long cotton skirt gathered at the waist with elastic. I thought that must be good for peeing in the woods. When I finished my cerveza con limon, I got on the road and I passed up Geraldine again. I saw a really cool church with three bell towers Then I noticed the giant nest at the top. Was that a stork? There was a farm house and field right next to the church.

Surprisingly, I caught up with Miranda from Holland. As we walked together, we enjoyed talking about our lives. She showed me a picture of her boyfriend. I told her I was leery of getting a boyfriend because I didn't want to be anyone's maid. She said that he does the laundry. They both take care of the home. I told her she was lucky. We walked down a hill into a town with a great view of modern suburbia, España style, with freeways and modern buildings mixed with ancient roads and buildings. I told her how much I hated to pee in the woods. She was indignant. She said, "What do you think, that you have something that I don't have? It's not a problem to pee in the bushes; everyone has to do it. You should get over it." I told her that in the USA it was against the law to expose yourself. We walked into a town and stopped at a bar. I remembered that she had no more money because she had used her last coin at the albergue to wash her clothes with me. I got her a cafe con leche. I was thinking about Carol and Karen and the salad they shared with me as well as Liam's beer and snacks. Later, as we walked further, we came to a bank. I waited while she used the ATM. Then she insisted on paying me back. We walked by an abandoned restaurant and she went into the patio to wee. I could see her through the fence. She was helping me gather nerve so I could stop being embarrassed.

We walked along together until we got to the cathedral in León. Then she kept going and I went to find my albergue, the Monastery San Francisco. It was a giant modern building. I got a room for the weekend. Mother's Day would be on Sunday. The monk took my passport and credential and he gave me my stamp. I bought breakfast and dinner for each day I was there. He gave me tickets and told me I would have to make reservations for each meal so they would know how much food to provide. My room was, thankfully, just one floor up. I was starting to feel weak. The room had a single bed, a night stand and a large desk by the window. The floor was linoleum. Everything was cream or beige. It had a private bathroom with a shower. I imagined these were perfect student's quarters.

I went to the cathedral when it opened at 4 pm. It had a museum attached to it. The cathedral had many side altars including one with a nativity and one with statues of the Holy Family. A large patio area outside had amazing statues and bas reliefs around the perimeter. I smiled and felt love in my heart for a wonderful statue of an angel with a gregarious laughing smile. In the center were enormous cone-shaped carved monoliths from antiquity, maybe the Mycenaean Civilization. On the way back to the monastery, I stopped at the pharmacy and got some cold medicine and vitamins.

Before dinner, I went down to the cafeteria. The big glass door was locked. They wouldn't let us in until exactly meal time. There were lots of orange tables and yellow and green chairs with an aisle up the middle. When the door opened, I went up past the tables, where there was a cafeteria line. The cook served each person's plate. There was a bowl with pieces of fruit and some yogurt to pick up at the end. The food at the monastery was great. I was used to eating lots of vegetables.

That night, I started feeling really weak and tired. When I went to breakfast, I sat by myself so I wouldn't get anyone else sick. I noticed that most of the other people were isolating too. Maybe everyone was sick. I went to a store to get some salt to gargle with. I picked up a few foods to enjoy, including strawberries, because it was Mother's Day, after all.

I slept most of Mother's Day. Down at the entry office, I paid for a couple of extra days so I could recuperate. I started making my skirt. I got my fingernail scissors and cut up my yoga pants leaving the hip pocket intact all the way up to the waist band. I cut the legs into 2 sections. They would be separated and sewn together and then gathered and sewn onto the top. I had the thread that I bought at the hardware store in Sahagún and a needle I brought from home in my minimal sewing kit. While I recuperated, I sewed my skirt together, one stitch at a time, with a blanket stitch hoping that would help it not fall apart. The skirt came together. I was missing my iron and big scissors which would have made it a lot easier. It was a little short in the front, but It was okay, I was pleased. I wore long socks and below-the-knees tights with the skirt. They covered my legs completely and were comfortable. I started feeling better around noon on Monday after Mother's Day.

The next day, I went out to a laundromat that I remembered passing on a previous shopping trip. I did my laundry; but I washed my skirt by hand in my bathroom sink. I did not want it to fall apart.

I went out again to find a post office. My google maps led me across town. I saw many stylish modern apartment buildings. One was circular with graphics of diamonds painted gold and green. Another was peach colored and light blue. I walked by a park that felt cool and was deep green under tall trees. Google took me to the address of where Siri said the post office was. The building said Correo on the door but it wasn't open. I was thinking that it was an industrial location, not an office where customers could buy stamps. I walked around, searching a bit, and saw a well-dressed woman sitting at a bus stop. I asked her where a post office was. She said, "No hablo Ingles." I looked up on my phone how to say it in Spanish. I asked her in Spanish. She looked at me, took a deep breath, and started speaking in English. She said, "Well, if you're going to try that hard..." She took me to the post office which was on the next street. I told her that she was my angel; she smiled and left. I hoped she didn't miss her bus. I inquired about a postal bag, that Greg told me about in Sahagan, to send some things home, but the lady didn't know what I was talking about. I got some stamps and I mailed my postcards.

My last night at the monastery, I was feeling pretty good. At dinner, after I got my food, I felt like I wanted some conversation. I spoke loudly from the front of the cafeteria and asked if anyone spoke English. Two men raised their hand. I went over and asked them if I could sit with them. They said yes. They were brothers and were walking a section of the Camino together. This was their last night together. We talked a lot and I'm sure I spoke too much. It was their last night together after all. I just needed to talk after being cooped up so long.

I left in the morning after breakfast. I felt like I needed to get away from my sick room. I made a reservation at another recommended albergue in Leon.

I let google maps find it for me. It was a big white house in a neighborhood. It was up from the street up a zig-zagged red stairway with a black iron gate and railing. I got there early so I decided to just sit on the steps and rest. A young woman arrived and she invited me in. Her name was Maria. I told her that I could wait outside until the albergue opened at 2. She told me, "No" and wanted me to come in and make myself at home. I went in and up the stairs. I found a lower bunk in one of the bunk rooms. The bunks were different prices depending on how many beds were in the room. There were two bunk beds in the room I chose. I thought maybe with fewer beds I would have less of a chance of having a snorer. The top bunk of the other bed in my room had a sleeping South Korean man.

All the doors had a sign that told what the room was, Kitchen, Living room, Garden, Laundry. The two restrooms had signs. One said Hombres and the other said Mujeres. Every time I went into the Mujeres room, the seat was up.

At two o'clock I went down and Maria signed me in and stamped my credential. The sign-in was at a dining room table in the lounge, which had a sofa and chairs, large round coffee table, a shelf of games, and a magazine rack. No meals were provided, so I went out to find food to cook. It's dangerous for me to eat at a restaurant in the land of bread and pasta.

I found a green grocer and got fruits and vegetables. Next door was a butcher. I got salami, pate with a green crust on it, chicken, and a special delightful semi soft sharp cheese. I was also looking for a mechanical pencil. All the ones I found had .5 lead. I cannot write with .5 lead. I looked all over town in all the shops I could find. I asked everyone. Finally, one man told me to go to the university bookstore. He said if I walked down the street in front of his shop, I would get there but it was far. I walked and walked through neighborhoods until I got to the university. I loved being near the university, which had a lot of young people on the street and in the bars and stores. Yes, the bookstore had the pencil I needed. I stopped in a bar and got a beer with lemon before heading back. Victory!

When I got back, I noticed another South Korean man sleeping in the lower bunk next to mine. I stowed my food in the fridge and ate some salami, cheese, and a peach.

I went up to the cathedral de Leon again for a final look. It was quite festive out on the street. There was a little train that carried passengers, mostly children, the length of the cathedral area. The bar across from the cathedral was burgeoning with tables and umbrellas. I sat a while and had a café con leche. I needed to rest. It felt good to relax among the patrons of the bar. I gave a 2-euro coin and a medal that I didn't need to a man who was sitting by the road holding a dish out. He thanked me profusely. I walked back to my albergue past the lovely ancient architecture of the town. I loved the giant Roman rock wall; it must have been 12 feet tall. The rocks were baseball sized field stones. It followed a path for what seemed blocks. I found a hiking shop and got another set of pole ends. Mine were worn through on two sides. I passed a colorful art fair that was being taken down. Sadly, I missed it.

There was yet another man sleeping in the bunk above me when I got back. He was ill. I was the only woman in the whole house that night. The new guy was French. I went into the kitchen to make dinner. I cooked onion, garlic, zucchini, red pepper, and chicken. I boiled eggs for the next day. I had strawberries for dessert.

That night while we were all trying to sleep, one of the South Korean men started to snore. The other South Korean man got up, shook him, and told him to stop. I thought, *What a great idea!*

In the morning I went down to the kitchen to make breakfast. The smiling French man was making his breakfast too. It looked and smelled good. I imagined he was a French chef. I went into the lounge and one of the South Korean men was working on his laptop computer. He said he had to still do his business on the Camino. It would take him just a little while and he would be off.

CHAPTER 13

LEAVING LEON

470 KM

I found the Camino by going to the cathedral. On the way, I passed a lovely small butter-yellow church aside the hill that led up to the cathedral. It seemed amazing that there was a church so close to the cathedral. Past the cathedral, I spied some yellow arrows leading away in a direction I hadn't been. I passed a marker that read 360 km to Santiago. I passed a series of pergolas, each surrounded with beautiful wisteria that seemed to go on forever, they waved in the breeze like purple and white foam. My heart loved it. I walked by a university that had shells for the Camino in a design all over the building. A larger-than-life-sized bronze statue of a peregrino was in the square. He was sitting with his shoes off and holding his wrist and his belly and leaning back as if asleep. I could relate. Past the university was a river. I walked over the bridge feeling free, but my backpack felt heavy on me. I walked through downtown watching for arrows. I only had 7 km to walk until La Virgin del Camino.

I walked through the outskirts of town and through an industrial area, past large factories. There was even a large building that said Porsche on it. The hills past the industrial area were a neighborhood of bodegas. The street I was walking on had doorway after doorway coming out of a hill. Some looked well-kept like someone used them. Others were dirty and unkept like they had been forgotten. Some had stairs going down to a door, others you had to step up to go in. There was an amazing one that looked like a modern house with a nice car in the driveway and a regular garage door but the back end of the house was a hill. There was a TV antenna out the top of the hill. I walked past the bodega hills and up through a neighborhood of normal houses toward a freeway. I walked along the freeway that turned into a mountain road. The topography was back country with pine trees and sporadic roadside businesses. I love pine trees. The white crunchy sandy dirt on the shoulder of the road was in high contrast to the dark green trees.

I came upon the town La Virgin del Camino abruptly. It seemed like a small town but the road was long from the beginning until I got to the turn off to the albergue. I turned left and followed the road across the railroad tracks and past lovely homes. I had good directions and the streets had signs; how nice. The monastery had a fence of large bushes so I couldn't tell where the entrance was. All of a sudden, I was there. I turned in and went down a cement path past a large grassy area with rows of clothes lines full of clothes. The entrance had benches before it. I walked through a glass door that was held open with a chair. A sign pointed to the check in room. I was glad they had a bottom bunk for me. The bunk room was massive. I stowed my gear, took a shower, washed my clothes in the sink in the bathroom, and hung them on the line. I laid my shower shoes out on a bench to dry. It was 81 degrees F, so they dried fast, as did my clothes.

I left to go food shopping at almost 5 when the supermercado opened. I inquired on the high road and someone told me where the mercado was, but when I got there, it was closed. I asked some teenage-looking women where another supermercado was. They told me to go down three blocks and turn right. It would be on my right another block down. They were right! It was a much nicer mercado and bustling inside. The fruit and veggies looked fresh. I got an apple and two bananas as well as potato to nuke in the morning. I also got eggs, a red pepper and a tomato for lunch, and some corn nuts. Six eggs were perfect: two for dinner, two for breakfast, and two for lunch. When I got back, everyone was making dinner. There were a lot of families and couples. People were cooking and eating together. Some women were cooking for their families. I cooked my food and sat and ate with everyone else. I cleaned up and went to bed. The snoring was deafening. After a while I got up and made myself some tea. I spied the couches in the lounge and got my sleeping bag and slept on a couch, but not for long.

The early-bird pilgrims were up at 5 making breakfast. I walked tired that day.

A giant mosaic announced Villar de Mazarife. The albergue looked like a small house with grass out front. Pilgrims were sitting at tables on the porch and grass, drinking wine and talking and laughing. I went in and stood in line to get my bunk for the night. The bunks were oddly situated two by two in the middle of the room and there were a few on the wall that were by themselves. I didn't want to sleep right next to someone I didn't know, so I made sure I got one by the wall. I went outside and sat at a table. Someone poured me a glass of wine. I wasn't sure how clean the glass was. The wind picked up, glasses and bottles were blowing off the tables! It was almost time for the store to open, so I walked down past the church to the stores. The church was on a hill. There were three storks' nests on the three bell towers. I marveled and wondered how the baby stork chicks could sleep when the bells tolled every 15 minutes all day long and at Mass times. A statue of a pilgrim stood in front of the church.

I looked into the first store I saw and the lady told me she wasn't opened yet. So, I went to the second one. I looked to see if there was something I could eat. I found some dried figs, dried peaches, and corn nuts. I had become fond of corn nuts, not something I usually eat. I went back to the other store, got some veggies, and I found a bottle of wine called Peregrino. It was only one euro. I got it. I hoped it would be good.

Back at the albergue, I sat out on the porch and opened my bottle of wine with the corkscrew on my swiss army knife. I shared it with two men and a couple who were sitting near. It was good, thank God. Dinner was announced, and I left the bottle out on a bench between two pillows so it wouldn't blow away. I traipsed down the stairs to the dining room. I was a bit tipsy, since I'm a lightweight where wine is concerned; so, I held onto the stair rail. I sat at an empty table and waited for people to sit down around me. A group of seven men sat across from me, a man at the end of the table, and another next to me. A fun young woman sat next to me on my other side. Each course of the dinner was served cafeteria style. We got up and stood in line for our food. It was a lot of good exercise. The wine at the table was red or white. I love a smooth dry red wine. I didn't want my head to come down; I was having too much fun. The man way at the other end of the long table was our host. He told the story of the albergue and his family. He loved sponsoring the albergue even though it was a lot of work for his family.

After dinner, I spoke to the man in the bed on the wall behind me. He was French. He said he walked a special longer Camino from northern France through a beautiful and perilous countryside. A man from South Korea chimed in and said he tried to go that way, but it was too much for him. The French guy drew a map for me to show me where his trail was.

I was hoping that having a lot of wine would help me sleep. I went to bed. I heard no snoring. Thank you, God. In the morning I got on the road early, munching my breakfast as I walked.

On the way to Hospitál de Órbigo, I saw a water tower with a stork nest on it. No shortage of storks here. Walking into town, there were a lot of shops. Then there was a long stone bridge over a grassy area that my book said was used for jousting in the middle ages. The place looked regal. I spied a building across the bridge that was painted large squares in orange, purple, and brown. I wondered if that was my albergue, but no. I was going to albergue Verde. It had a relaxing "Hippie" atmosphere. I walked into a large garden and up some wooden stairs to a door with a whimsical twisting metal and rainbow patina door knob. Inside a man was at a desk in the middle of the room checking people in. On the far side of the room was a sharing pit lined with pillows and bean bag chairs. It was very colorful. The volunteer, Carina, was a fun lady in colorfully embroidered clothing. They didn't take money. We were to donate in a box on the table before we left in the morning. I got a lower bunk by a window with white linen embroidered curtains. The lady in the bunk next to mine was from North Carolina. She was going home the next day. She had one week to walk and her week was over. She was talking to her family a lot on her phone. I think she had teenagers at home.

The bathroom wasn't co-ed. Everything was clean and well-kept. I washed my clothes out in the sink in the garden after my shower. I hung them on the line with everyone else's. At first, I marveled at how I always got all my clothes back after hanging them with everyone else's but now I expect it. Everyone pains-takingly selected each piece of clothing for their trek. Everyone knows their clothes, and no one wants to carry more than they have to.

I sat on the grass and looked for four-leaf clovers. I remembered my Aunt Loretta used to have a collection of four-leafed clovers. She told me that I didn't have time to look for them though. I had chores and school work to do. I figured it was my time now to look for them. There were two dachshunds in the garden. They were very social and wanted me to watch them. The guy dog kept coming up to me and sitting on my lap and putting his head under my hand. When he jumped down to run around, the other dog replaced him on my lap, when he noticed this, he nudged her off. Sheesh. A lady came out and tried to get them to leave me alone. The masseuse arrived. I signed up for a massage. She used a downstairs room. It was good to have a massage.

Dinner was family style. A chef came and made a gourmet vegetarian dinner for us. There was some kind of special drink and special soup, pasta, and veg-etables. Carina sang grace at the beginning of dinner.

She had a beautiful voice. We sat around and talked in the sharing pit after dinner. That night there was snoring. I got up and pushed on a snoring man and told him to stop snoring. He said okay, but he didn't stop. Ugh. When I woke up, he had left already. Breakfast was all over the tables in the morning. The bread was big and made wonderful toast. There were bags of cereal, butter, honey, and jams on the tables and beautiful blue and green ceramic bowls plates and cups. The chef left the coffee ready to plug in.

Leaving the albergue Verde was a bit uncomfortable. They told us to go out the back gate and walk across a field as a short cut. I didn't feel comfortable walking across someone's field. Besides, there were no arrows in the field and I didn't know where to exit the field to find the Camino. So, I took a farm road between the albergue and the field. I walked to the main drag and turned left, hoping I would find the yellow arrows soon. Yes! I was glad to see a yellow arrow.

I walked through farm country. No uphills, yay. The Camino found its way through small farming communities each with its own set of amenities: a high school, a park, a conclave of factories, play grounds, swimming pools, and always a church. I walked through a neighborhood with sidewalks, always following the arrows. It was important to be on the correct side of the street or it was easy to miss an arrow. It was great to walk by people just living their lives: neighbors being neighborly, children playing in the garden, someone walking fast, someone walking slow. I stopped into a bar and ordered tortilla, a piece of quiche filled with eggs and lots of potatoes and onion. Whenever I asked if it had milk, they always said no. A lot of times at home, the scrambled eggs have milk. I walked out of the towns and into the country side. I saw a giant pillar with a vertical graphic of two hands clasped at the wrist. Dramatically, it was about 20 feet high and it took up the whole pillar.

I came to a rest area "provided with love." It was a series of booths surrounded with colorful tapestries. There were couches to sit on. They served fruit and tea on a table in one of the booths. They didn't want any money. Pilgrims milled around conversing and resting. I asked a man to take my picture. He did and then he came over to me and put his arm around me, smiled, and took a selfie with me. I remember him still when I see that picture.

CHAPTER 14

ASTORGA

518 KM

Walking into Astorga was a delight. Homes had whimsical art in their yards and on their houses. Right as I turned a corner, a house had a wooden cut out of a peregrino painted black like a silhouette high on their fence. The next house had a motif of a stylized spider web over part of their windows. One had wooden cutouts of black cats playing on a green picket fence. I started seeing really big signs of the Camino on cement beside the walkway. One was a yellow arrow on a blue field and another was the stylized shell motif.

The place where I stayed in Astorga was a convent run by nuns and volunteers. When I got there, the line was out the door. I patiently waited hoping they wouldn't run out of beds before they got to me. When it was my turn I asked if I could stay for 2 nights because I wanted to go to Mass on Sunday. The nun who was signing us in told me yes. She took my passport and credential. She wrote very slowly all the information she needed and gave me my stamp. The first night I was on the top floor and there was no elevator. The second day I was lucky to be there early and I got to be on the entry floor. Not so much climbing. The later you get there, the higher up in the building you get. Also, the colder the shower will be. One thing I worried about before the Camino was cold showers.

The wise know that when you get to an albergue, take your shower right away before everyone else uses up the hot water. Also, wash your clothes so they'll have time to dry. I was usually worn out when I arrived, fell into my bed, and took a nap first. My bunk room filled up fast. A Camino-made family of young men and women from different countries was in my room. They spoke French and English. They seemed comfortable with each other. One man came into the room with wet hair and someone asked him if the shower was cold. He said, "almost, but not quite." At that point, I decided I'd better get my shower before it got all the way cold. That was the coldest shower I had on the Camino, and it wasn't quite cold. The lady on the bunk above mine was walking alone too. We talked for a while.

I went out and got some food at the supermercado. Across from the convent was a big neighborhood of tall close buildings. It seemed like they were attached but there were lanes to walk between them. If I put my hands out, I could touch both walls. Past that was a large plaza as big as three football fields with shops all around. The supermercado was at the far end. It was really huge. It had a bakery, a butcher shop, and a produce shop. You could get all kinds of food there. Since I was staying two nights, I got chicken to cook twice and eggs and my favorite vegetables and a potato to take with me when I left. I got some bacon for breakfast. I looked at the wine and decided on the one called Peregrino since I had good luck with that brand the last time. The checkout man seemed pleased that I had my own bags. I enjoyed my walk back to the convent because there were a lot of dress shops in the plaza area. I love to look at fashion.

The kitchen was at the bottom of the house downstairs from the entry. I made my dinner and took it to the table where the group from my room where eating together. One of the women was telling the others to speak in French so she could understand them. A French man scolded her telling her to grow up and learn English so she could talk to everyone. The group had an American and a German man who spoke English so English was the language that was spoken. Of course, it was more fun for me when people spoke English. I brought out my wine. I tried it. It wasn't very good. The others tried it and told me to dump it out and have some of theirs. I asked at the table if anyone would like some bad wine because I was going to dump it. An older Spanish man on the other side of me said he would take it. I said, "really?" He got a glass and poured it and drank it while staring at his food, oh my! It was great to be included in their group. I cleaned up our dishes and went to bed ahead of them, hoping to get to sleep before the snoring.

In the morning, before 8:00, the volunteer told me that I would have to leave the albergue and return later to sign in. They let me leave my pack in a room downstairs. I went looking for a church to go to Mass. I went to the closest one on my Mass app but it was farther than indicated and I was late. The other churches were too far away. I saw a bunch of people in front of a church but it turned out they were just leaving. I asked someone where the next Mass was. They told me about a church nearby. I went there and was on time for an intimate Mass service. The church was small and had a beautiful and simple altar of gold and white diamond shapes. I was conscious of my pilgrim clothes in a church of well-dressed people. I wondered how the church parishioner thing worked in these towns that have so many churches. In California, we live in parishes that encompass miles of homes. Here, a church is on every fifth corner.

After Mass, I went back to the convent and I tried to stand below the steps at the entrance before it was time to check in. I didn't want to get into a big long line later. A custodian came out and told me to go away and come back later. I walked around in the park behind the convent. It was stark with few trees. It had white quartz rock beds around displays with signs about historical happenings in Astorga. I took a walk around the buildings across from the convent. I enjoyed seeing people do the things they do in Astorga Spain. I got a cup of coffee and some pastry at a shop on the plaza. I also bought a lovely tin of cookies that had a painting of the Camino map and it had Camino Santiago written on it as part of the design.

The next time I went to the convent, there was a line, and a sister let us in. I went to get my backpack and was watched carefully by a volunteer as I retrieved it. They weren't casual about protecting the other backpacks in the room. Since I was among the first pilgrims checking in, I got my bunk on the first floor. A middle-aged woman who was walking the Camino with her elderly father claimed an upper bunk across the room. She seemed to be an executive type. She had everything organized and spoke pleasantly and efficiently. It was uplifting because she seemed pleased with everything. She showed me her towel. It was a lightweight synthetic shammy that she got from a relative. She said she tried many different kinds of towels and settled on that one. She was going to take a nap while her dad explored the town. A young Frenchman was there with his girlfriend. He took a nap too. It was easier to sleep in the day than at night with the snoring.

I took my clothes down to the laundry. I tried to buy soap in the machine, but it didn't work. A volunteer told me to go and buy some soap from the sister. Up I went to find her. She kindly didn't make me wait in line behind all the pilgrims. I gave her my euros and she gave me a little box. She said it was enough soap to do about three loads. Down at the laundry, I put my clothes in the washer and some coins and let the washer do its thing. The clotheslines were on the patio. I used my safety pins to hang the clothes and made sure to position them so they would be in the breeze. I made my lunch and ate it on the patio. The view was expansive across the valley and low hillside past the roofs of the closer buildings and church in town. The landscape, under a blue sky, was surprisingly dry and yellow-green with a few green trees and some clusters of houses and some roads. Rain clouds hung low in the distance. It was beautiful. After lunch, I left the convent to explore.

I found a store with hiking poles in a bin outside and packs in the window. I went into the hippy-decorated shop to find a small pack to carry my day things in when I shuttled my pack. It had to be very light and have a waist strap and hopefully a chest strap. All the ones I saw weighed too much and had no extra straps. It was obviously a gift shop, not a hiking shop. Sadly, I went to leave, but I saw a stairway going down. Another shop was downstairs! It was a real hiking store. I looked and looked and finally found a really light pack that stuffed into a little pouch. Perfect, now I needed to find some straps. I asked the man behind the counter. He had strap material on a bolt so I could buy as much as I needed. I would sew the straps on. He also had clips to close the straps! I had him measure me for how much I would need. The whole thing, pack, and straps, cost less than 20 euro. I was happy. I walked out beaming at my victory. As I walked past the plaza, I saw more interesting shops: a candy store with a taffy pulling machine in the window and with a soda fountain set up inside, a cigar store, and a real estate office. It was interesting to see what real estate was available.

I went down a tree-lined street with historic markers and rest areas. I saw a grey stucco beautiful castle designed by Gaudi. It was whimsical and grand. It was opened but going to close in 30 minutes. I looked at the times it would be opened again but they were after I would be gone. Past the castle was the cathedral, also grand. I walked around the splendid grounds. It looked like an elegant gold-colored fortress with gardens and patios behind a high iron gate.

A pilgrims' blessing would be given that evening at the church across from the convent. I knew that I needed all the blessings I could get. When I entered the church, I couldn't miss a large picture of handsome Jesus. He had a great smile, chin-length scruffy hair, and was reaching out with his hand with an obvious nail hole in it. Many colorful professionally made signs were around the church. I don't know what they all said but some of them were about loving and caring and understanding others. The peregrinos gathered near the altar and a small man handed out the pilgrim blessing from a box; each colored paper was printed in a different language. This is the English translation. I have copied it here, word for word:

The BENEDICTION, English
O Lord, you who from the beginning of times
Guided the steps of men,
You who called Abraham out of his land
To lead him into the promised land;
You who protected with your benevolence
To those who guided by you,
Have made this pilgrimage to Santiago.
We pray for you to watch this pilgrim, who,
For the love of your name, make a pilgrimage to
Santiago de Compostela.
Be for them, a companion on our journey, the
guide on our Intersections
The strengthening during fatigue,
the fortress in danger
The resource on our itinerary,
the shadow in our heat
The light in our darkness,
the consolation during dejection

And the power of our intention.
So that we under your guidance, Lord,
May reach the end of our journey
And strengthened in faith, happy in hope,
and generous in love;
May come back to their home healthy and
full of your spirit.
For Jesus Christ, Our Lord.
Iglesia Perpetuo Socorro – Astorga

The translation was rough in grammar. We were blessed by the monsignor with much ceremony, care, and love and we were sent on our way full of the graces of the blessing. I took a picture of my blue blessing paper and put it back in the box

It was too late to get my bottle of wine at the supermercado so I stopped and got a glass of wine at a bar. I hoped the wine would help me not be bothered by snoring.

That night, in stark contrast to the night before, I ate alone out on the patio. I asked a young man if I could sit with him. He said yes, but his girlfriend showed up unhappy and he moved to another table to eat alone with her. He came over and apologized later when he saw me in the kitchen. One thing I liked about walking the Camino alone was that there was no drama. More importantly, there was no one for me to complain to. I just had to meet every experience as it came and make sense of it for myself. I decided that I wanted another glass of wine, so I walked down to the bar after dinner, but it was closed.

The executive lady snored loudly, ugh. In the morning I packed up and set aside the things in my pack that I didn't need like my: halfway certificate that I got in Sahagún, the headlight that I never used, a blow-up washing bowl, and the tin of cookies I just bought. I went down to the kitchen to nuke my potato. The lady who cleaned the kitchen caught me being there past 8 am. I had my potato in the microwave for 4 minutes and had to wait for it. She told me to get out. I pointed to the microwave. She put her hands on her hips and glared at me till the microwave beeped. I took my potato out, wrapped it in my bandana, and stowed it in my bag. She threw up her hands and kept saying loudly "Madre de Dios, Madre de Dios" repeatedly. I didn't get if she were yelling at me or herself.

Walking out of town was bittersweet. Astorga was a wonderful place with a lot of amenities for pilgrims. I felt comfortable there at the convent. I needed to be on my way. Nothing much was going on in town that early, the plaza was almost empty. I walked by the post office. It was open. I went in to see if I could send a package home. The lady at the counter said she didn't speak English well. Between my little Spanish and her little English, we got the package sent. She brought me an international mailing bag. She asked me if there were any lithium batteries. I forgot about the headlamp and said no (the headlamp didn't make it home.) It was 45 euro to send my stuff home. That was a lot. I lightened my pack by a kilo and a half. That was good.

As I walked by, I noticed the cathedral door was open and people were entering. They were just starting Mass so I went in. The Mass was in one of the side altars close to the front. It was like a little chapel within the big church. I could see how grand the cathedral was. There were some crippled people and just regular people and older people as well as prominent looking people. I blended in well. I had my pack and poles.

I didn't want to stow my poles by the wall because I didn't want to forget them. So, I kept all my clunky stuff near me. My heart loved being there.

I walked out of the cathedral and followed a yellow arrow that sent me around the stone-walled corner and down a road that revealed a neighborhood that wasn't as grand as Astorga proper. I saw a beautiful modern church. Further down, there was a man outside of a restaurant. He was sharpening knives. I asked him if he would sharpen my Swiss Army knife. He said yes. I waited a bit until he was finished with what he was doing. He sharpened my knife. Wow, he really took off a lot of metal. It wasn't as pretty as it used to be, but at least it was sharp. I gave him the 5 euros he charged me. The neighborhood turned into the countryside with buildings further apart.

A bright blue sign had a picture of the stylized shell and arrow pointing up in yellow. It led the way. The climate was drier. A low rock wall straddled a wide dirt road. I looked out over the rough chaparral with a lonely tree far off and mountains even farther. Clouds were wafting across the pale blue sky. Coming into a town down a dirt road with rock walls on each side, the church was the first thing visible in the town. I walked by a fence of rotting wood that had been painted many colors but was faded and mostly not painted anymore. Maybe they took discarded wood from many fences to make that little one.

CHAPTER 15

GUACELMO

540 KM

Walking on, I saw another white horse in a field with cattle. The trail led me to Rabanal del Camino, a little town. Many of the structures were built using an ancient building and then adding on to it with new construction like new terracotta bricks next to old somewhat crumbling brown bricks. The old part of a building might have crooked lines and the new part had straight lines. There were ancient stone walls around gardens. I walked into town asking people where the address of my albergue was, and they pointed, leading me in the right direction. I went by little stores and other businesses. The streets seemed to wind around. I was staying at Refugio Guacelmo where English volunteers made English tea at 4:30 each afternoon. A monastery was next door. They had vespers at night with Gregorian Chant in Latin in the church across the plaza. When I arrived at Guacelmo, they were checking pilgrims in. We stood in the garden and the line sort of went up the terra cotta stairs. I got in line. I ended up in a bunkhouse near the garden. I got my lower bunk. The bunkhouse had two rooms. Very few pilgrims in the rooms weren't South Korean. The bathrooms were in the big house. I went in and showered and washed my clothes. Many clotheslines were in the extensive garden out back with plenty of clothespins so I used them to hang my clothes with the others. It was fairly windy, which would help them dry before long. I found a lounge chair on the grass and stretched out, thinking that I could possibly come out there to sleep if there were snoring. I went to the grocery store when it opened. I got veggies, eggs, fruit and a potato to nuke in the morning. I got a bottle of wine, thinking it would help me sleep.

When I got back, it was almost tea time. It was also sharing time. We sat at a large square table on the patio with benches all around so that the pilgrims in the corner couldn't get out without making everyone move. I sat on the outside away from the table because the chairs near the table were full. While we shared, a pot of hot sweet tea was brought out with biscuits and a lot of little cups. When empty, the pot was taken back in to make more tea. We went around the table and each of us shared or not. Everyone's willingness to share made me willing to share too. And those who sat back and said pass were respected. The proprietor shared that the Refugio Guacelmo was operated by the kind hospitaleros associated with the Confraternity of Saint James in the UK. He said that he really liked it when people followed the rules. Tea at 16:30, vespers in Latin chant 19:00, pilgrims blessing at 21:30. Door closes at 22:00. Lights out at 22:30, breakfast of bread & jam and butter 6:30. Be gone at 8:00

It was interesting to me that he said that the United States had decided that they were too far away to sponsor an albergue so they donated money to a fund that helped support repairs on albergues that were struggling. There was an association among the albergues that oversaw repairs and made sure each albergue maintained a healthy environment. Sometimes a roof was replaced with the funding or bunkbed or shower repairs or any repair that was applied for and approved. There was some discussion about who could stay at this albergue. They didn't accept backpacks from the shuttle services. They had standards for pilgrims. We had to be carrying our packs with us. They didn't allow people who arrived in vehicles. They did allow people who were sick to stay even if they had to come in a cab. I had been thinking of having my pack transported the next day because I was feeling weak still from my illness and the next day would be a long trek. One of the volunteers told us about breakfast. It would be out on the patio. No one would be allowed in the kitchen in the morning. I asked one of the volunteers if I would be allowed to microwave my potato in the morning. She said no. They would be using the kitchen in the morning to prepare breakfast for us and pilgrims in the kitchen would be inconvenient. She came to me later and apologized but she said it wasn't allowed.

I went into the kitchen to see what it was like. It was a cozy white room with 8 red and white plaid oil-cloth clad tables spaced out in the middle of the room. Towards the wall with windows, there were a couple of stoves. And on another wall, near the sink, were the cupboards for dishes and silverware and utensils. Pots and pans were stowed in lower cabinets. The refrigerators were on another wall. There was some activity in the kitchen with people starting to make their dinner: a family from Sri Lanka, and two guys from Spain. I started preparing my meal. I was frying my onion and zucchini in butter. I cut up tomatoes and was about to put them in my pot when a man turned off my burner and took my pot off the stove. I told him to stop. He said it was too dry, I poured my tomatoes into it, turned it back on, and told him it would be fine. I guess he was trying to help or he wanted the burner. People are funny. About that time the kitchen was hopping with pilgrims fixing their dinner on the counter and around the tables. I spied a table with an empty chair, I asked the family if I could sit with them. The woman smiled and nodded. They didn't speak English and I didn't speak their language, but we smiled and nodded to each other during our feasting. After eating my delicious meal, I cleaned up and stowed my food in my bag in the fridge. I nuked my potato for the morning. It wouldn't be warming for me, but it would be cooked.

A woman told me that if I needed to have my bag transported, I should get an envelope from the hotel down the road and call the transport company and tell them to pick up my bag at the hotel and to tell them where I would be staying next. The hotel wasn't far away. I went and got my envelope. I called the company and set up my pickup and delivery. They said to have it downstairs at the hotel by 8 am. I went out, got my laundry off the line, and, soon, it was time for vespers across the street.

The church was simple, and the light was mostly from candles with a few overhead lamps. The chanters wore brown monk robes and sat in two rows facing each other in the front of the church. There was a sea of chairs with kneelers for the pilgrims. Still, there wasn't enough room for everyone. As more people arrived, they stood on the sides and in the back. I was glad to have a seat. As some of the monks came in late and took their places up front and started singing, the sound got bolder. There were leaflets of the prayers so we could chant with them. Being 69, I was raised in the Latin tradition of the Catholic Church. The Latin vespers were a bit familiar to me. When I was in 6th grade, my school choir was trained to chant the requiem Mass in Latin. Many of the words and melodies were awakened in my memory. I loved it.

It was time to sleep when we returned to the albergue. I got my pack ready for the morning, put my 5 euros in the envelope, and attached it to my pack. I snuggled down in my sleeping bag and said my rosary. The lady above me started snoring very loud first. I got up and told her to turn over and stop snoring. She did. Then the guy across from me started snoring. I fumed. When he snored, I made a loud snoring sound. He stopped and looked at me. Then he went back and started snoring again. I made a loud noise again. We did this for a long while. I thought about the lounge chair in the garden. I went out there but some pilgrims were having a party, drinking wine and laughing. I went to the patio and laid on one of the benches by the square table. I got about 2 hours of sleep before the early risers started making noise. I got everything together, putting the things I would need for the day in my little pack and my purse bag and I left for the hotel. As I was leaving, the head volunteer saw me and he noticed the envelope attached to my pack. He raised his eyebrows. I got out of there. There's a lot of discussion among pilgrims that it's not good to judge someone else's Camino. We all do the best we can at all times. This group wanted to serve only hard-working pilgrims. To myself, in my defense, I felt good that I let myself get help with my pack because I was still weak from being sick and not getting sleep.

CHAPTER 16

BIRTHDAY

554 KM

It was a perilous climb to La Cruz De Ferro. This is a giant cross on a hill where pilgrims leave a stone that they brought from home. A lady from Iceland and I took pictures of each other on the hill below the cross. I left three heart-shaped stones and put them in a row together. One was for me, one for my husband, and one for my mother. Many flowering bushes were near the trail and out on the hills, beautiful. A yellow flowering bush had a strong heavy smell, especially when it covered the entire hillside. Part of the trail led through thick flowered bushes that seemed to reach out and feel us as we walked. There was snow on far mountains that seemed close because we were so high up. I passed cattle in a field of chaparral and grass, their bells clinking as they ate. I walked up a mountain on a rocky path with a forest up ahead and pink heather clumps. It was so beautiful, yet so taxing, to walk uphill all day. I felt like I was at the top of the world looking out at purple mountains majesty in Spain. I stayed in Acebo, a town with two-story houses in stone and wood, each with a balcony in rough wood and iron. The houses lined the road leading into the town.

The next day was my 70th birthday. They said it would be difficult coming down the mountain, but the beauty would make up for it. They were right. Another day of "this cannot last forever" up-hills, ankle wrenching, broken slate striated trails, steep downhills, (I hate the feeling of my boot slipping over rock.) My angels did a good job keeping me vertical. Yay, angels of light! I made myself a corsage with flowers from the trail for my birthday. I had been getting myself a birthday corsage at a florist at home for years while I was caring for my husband. This year, I made my own. I walked by sheep and goats frolicking in a large hillside field. They even had one black sheep. I stopped into St. Sebastian Church along the way. It was small and had a wooden roof made of poles and planks. The inner church was surrounded by a rock wall on the bottom and white stucco on the top. The altar was red with painted vines encircling pillars. St. Sebastian was standing behind the cross over the altar. There was a statue of Mary holding Jesus on one side and another of Mary holding Jesus on the other. Four other saints' statues were above. The churches were usually closed unless, like this one, they had some sort of concession to employ a protector for the church. There was a little gift shop table at the back of the church. I knelt in a pew at the front of the church, said a quick rosary, and was off. Further on, I saw a remarkable house with creative steps. At the bottom, there was a block of cement. The next four steps were stones of different colors cut sharply into rectangles. The top three steps were wooden, with crutches at the first wooden one to hold it up. The house was rock and mortar at the bottom and wood and mud almost covering ancient bricks at the top. The balcony upstairs led to a front door. An ancient wooden garage door with spindles at the top was on the street floor.

Being out on the trail again was beautiful, with a winding dirt path surrounded by shrubbery, trees, and vines. There was no shortage of signs to lead the way along this stretch, one stating that this was the "Camino Frances" and another said, "To Santiago." I started seeing red poppies waving in the breeze again. I had missed them for a while. In a garden, a beautiful bush of roses cascading in profuse trusses was a lovely sight. The wilderness was beautiful too. Coming down the mountain, I saw Ponferrada in the distance. First, I saw a few newly built houses in a small neighborhood. Then there was a space with no buildings. Then I was in the town and the neighborhoods were close, street after street. I came to an ancient giant arch below a street. I wondered if it were the one that I had read about where sick pilgrims could go through to get their plenary indulgence if they couldn't make it to Santiago. I was feeling queasy and tired.

I followed the directions to my hotel where I had

a reservation. When I got there, the lady told me that they were full. I told her I had a reservation. I showed her in her book where they had written down my credit card number. I was getting worried. She called someone. She came back and erased my credit card number. She said she was sorry. I asked her what I should do. She led me to the bar and gave me a beer. She got on the phone and got me another room. It was more money, and I said that wasn't okay. She gave me 15 euros to make up the difference and gave me directions to the other hotel. I told her that it was my birthday and I had to have a bathtub. She assured me that it did.

I walked to the other hotel and started telling the lady that I had been sent there. She knew who I was. I told her I had to have a bathtub. She said they had no bathtubs. I told her it was my birthday and I had to have a tub. She contacted another hotel across town and assured me that they had tubs. So, I walked over there. When I got to the Hotel Alda, I was very tired. It was a nice modern hotel in the heart of downtown. It was actually less money than the second hotel. They took my information, but strangely, not my credit card info. A lady took me to my room up an elevator and up some stairs. The elevator stopped between every other floor so I had to either walk up to my floor or down. The room was small, but had a double bed, an armoire, a nightstand, and a desk. The bathroom had a bidet along with the tub and other standard equipment. I didn't know what to do with the bidet. Everything was modern and well maintained. I was so tired I wanted to lay down and not go to the supermercado to get bath salts and bubble bath. I ate a potato that I cooked three days before. I slept for a couple of hours and then went out to the store. I got some bath stuff with mineral salts. I got an eclair with pudding in it but I was thinking that I wanted some whipped cream too. I got some frozen stuff with a picture of strawberries on the package. I wondered if it was strawberry ice cream or frozen strawberries. It turned out to be whipped cream. So, yay for me! I ate my birthday treats, soaked in my tub, and went to sleep, shutting my eyes on my birthday.

The next day I just rested. I'd had the back-door trots for a few days. I started profusely coughing up yellow phlegm. I went to the pharmacy to see what they had for me. I was so tired. At the pharmacy I got a probiotic for my gut and some electrolyte powder and some medicine for my cold symptoms. I also got some yogurt drink at the supermercado, thinking that would help my gut. When I drank it my stomach hurt. What a bummer, maybe milk wasn't for me. I dumped it down the sink. I stayed in bed for the rest of the day. I ate an apple and it made me feel good. I found a use for the bidet. I washed my clothes in it.

I decided to stay in Ponferrada four nights to rest up and get well. The next day I forced myself to go out to visit the Templars Castle. Walking up to it was spectacular. It had flags on pinnacles and notched topped walls. The "Restoration and Historical Inquiry Efforts" yielded different and interesting building styles and materials from across the ages. They had many displays of period costumes of nobles, religious, peasants and merchants, war machines, writings, and writing equipment. I walked the ramparts and read the many signs about the history of the place. There were modern classrooms set up as rooms in the castle. Age-worn stone ledges for the guards to sit were situated next to the many ancient keyhole openings in the outside walls of the castle. They gave framed peaceful, idyllic, and beautiful views across the valley. At the bottom of the castle, a simple iron gate led out to a steep dirt trail down to the river far below where they got their water.

Across from the castle was a tapas bar. I wanted to go there for dinner but it didn't open until 8 pm and I was too tired to wait that long. I stopped into a Mediterranean restaurant in town and got shaved meat on a salad. I felt weak and like I needed more protein. On the way back to the hotel, I noticed that the supermercado was closed. I hoped they would have bottled water at the hotel. I went into the hotel bar and got a Dewars, hoping that would cure me somehow. The bartender didn't know what I wanted when I asked for a Dewars. I had to point to it for him. It wasn't until later that I was told that I should ask for a white label instead. I also got an agua grande at the bar. Then I got another good night's sleep.

The next morning, I went to the laundromat down the street. I noticed people were preparing for a big shindig in the cordoned-off street a block down from my hotel. They were setting up a dance floor, folding chairs, small tables, and big flat pans on giant portable stoves for cooking Paella. Back at my hotel bar, I got tortilla and café Americana for breakfast. Each time I went out the party in the street got more and more interesting. Little girls and their grown-up teachers started showing up dressed up in their flamenco dancing attire with their hair stylish and sprayed into place. Whole families were there, including grandparents. They sat at the tables on the side of the street and watched the dancing. It was very exciting for me to be there watching this delightful tradition. When the food was finally finished, I bought a plate of paella with chicken for lunch and sat in one of the chairs to watch the dancing.

I went to Mass up by the castle. It was in a large auditorium. The folk music with guitars and singers was rousing. The room was filled with folding chairs with an aisle up the middle. The priest came in with a procession up the middle and to the altar. There was a lot of singing and a lot of joy.

Afterward, I went to the tapas bar. It was opened. I went in and was told to sit anywhere. The restaurant had terracotta floors on two levels with a wooden fence in between. The chef brought me a bottle of wine and a menu. I selected my tapas. I was happy to see that everything had protein in it. I ordered locano with peppers, beef cheeks, mixed salad, strawberries, and sparkling water with lemon in the glass. He also brought me three colors of bread and thick balsamic vinegar and olive oil. The salad had smoked fish, very tender. The locano was their special thinly sliced smoked ham, with roasted and peeled large red peppers. The beef cheeks had potatoes. The strawberries were so sweet. There was no wait staff; the chef served me my food in stages on little plates, one at a time. A young couple came in when I was halfway through my meal. They sat at a booth near my table. It seemed like a special night for them, they were dressed elegantly. When my dinner was finished, I paid, thanked the chef and walked outside. The restaurant was up on a hill. I had a great view of the town of Ponferrada. Walking quite a distance back to the hotel, in the late dusk, using my google maps, was no problem.

I decided to walk the Camino the next day. It seemed like the more I laid around the more my back was hurting. My back usually doesn't hurt. I needed to renew my Vodaphone card and there was a Vodaphone store around the corner from my hotel. Monday morning, I got everything together and checked out of the hotel. At Vodaphone, the lady sold me a phone plan that had more data time for about half what I paid last time. That was good for me. She set it up.

CHAPTER 17

TODDLER BABY JESUS

585 KM

I was glad to be on the road after four days recuperating in Ponferrada. It was a warm day but the breeze was cool. Walking out of the town, the scenery turned into neighborhoods and then a university that was spaced out, modern and serene. The streets were wide and had fast traffic. Signs helped you know where to cross: a square blue sign with a white triangle and a person walking across a bunch of lines indicated to be careful and cross here. When I got past all that, I was on a country road with trees and houses far apart.

I walked by a church. The sign said, Santa Maria de Compostilla. It was painted with pictures of happy people, some playing music, some dancing. The churches were usually locked like this one was but I appreciated the joyful art on the outside walls. There was a sweet picture of Mary and St. Anna, her mother and a picture depicting the Annunciation. They were very descriptive, lovely pictures. As I went on, the vegetation got more abundant and I saw a creative new Camino sign. It was a tall rusty steel staff with a yellow shell at the top and a hand holding the staff with the pointer finger being a yellow arrow, amusing. I walked through a tunnel under a freeway. It was cool and quiet with graffiti covering the walls. I came to another church with a large painting on the side wall of a pilgrim relaxing. Next, fields of poppies on both sides of the trail gave accent to a few trees far off, with the mountains further and cumulous clouds hugging the mountains. I walked by a rock-walled rose garden. The trees were so full of roses, you could hardly see the leaves. There was a tall stately stone cross with Jesus on one side and a pilgrim on the other side. A church,

Iglesia de Santa Maria had an impressive ornate altar and the cutest ancient barefooted toddler baby Jesus statue standing smiling and giving a blessing. It also had an ancient 13th-century Mary the mother of God. The scene of the last supper was painted on the ceiling. The whole church was decorated with paintings on every wall and in every corner.

I stopped in a bar and got a cup of tea because I was feeling weak. I drank six cups of tea. I think I was dehydrated. The lady made my tea by shooting boiling water out of her expresso machine into my cup. I felt sorry that she had to keep doing that for me. It was interesting to see the personable barmaid; she was so friendly to everyone. She talked familiarly to old and young alike. Everyone liked her and was good-naturedly vying for her attention. When I left the bar, I noticed some modern sculptures near the sidewalk. There was a roughly hewn sculpture of a nude woman sitting straight up on a cement block with one leg down in a sitting position and the other knee bent up and her hands were on it under her chin. A low fountain gurgled next to her. Under a leafy vine-laden pergola was a sculpture of a standing woman with a long dress and with her hands at her sides and big hair. Walking out of town, I turned a corner and everything changed. I was in wine country. Apparently, you can grow grapes in a field of rocks. There were rows and rows of grapevines on both sides of the trail. My book told me that the region's microclimate was perfect for growing grapes.

Outside of Cacabelos was a park or service area. I couldn't wait to get to my albergue, so I trudged on. I stayed in Cacabelos. I had a private room at Hostel Santa Maria. Thankfully, the woman at the desk waited for me to get there. She checked me in, stamped my credential, gave me my key, and left. My room was small and had a view of the top of some buildings and a clothes line on the roof-deck below. I went out to get some food. I was trying to find food without milk in it. I thought vegetables and aioli would be good. As it turned out, the aioli had cream in it. I got some veggies and an apple at the mercado. When I got back to the hostel, my key didn't work on the entry door. I was glad that another woman was entering too. Her key worked. I decided to stay inside the rest of my time there. I needed to rest anyway. I went to the bar area where there was a microwave, hot water, tea and condiments for the pilgrims. I made many cups of tea with lemon wedges and some bouillon. A foursome of two couples was enjoying their evening together and another couple as well. I spent my time writing my Facebook entry to my friends who were praying for me and my WhatsApp entry to my children. My daughter, Carla, made a WhatsApp for my Camino trip called "Mom's walkabout check-in." I was sharing my more-gory and health-related details with my children. I got a good night's sleep and left early in the cool morning. It was lovely with birds chirping, and, as always, the day beckoned with the promise of a new adventure.

The following two days of so much uphill were too much. When I got up one hill, my ears didn't equalize for over half an hour. The scenery was beautiful, but the uphill was draining and exhausting.

I stopped on the downside of the mountain at Trabadelo. As I came into the albergue a lady was signing people in by a window to the side. I went in and discovered a walled garden with grassy areas. Lounge chairs and tables with chairs were set up around a cement patio with a sink for doing laundry. The kitchen had no cooking facilities. A restaurant/bar/mercado was next door. Upstairs was the bunkhouse. I got my bunk and went down to the store to see what was available. I got a couple of apples and ate a wilted lunch salad at the bar. I went up, took my shower, and then down to the patio to wash my clothes. After hanging them up, I sat in a lounge chair on the patio. A woman said she was going to go to the restaurant on the corner for dinner. We decided to go together. We went in but no one was in the restaurant. She decided not to wait around and left. I told her I wanted to wait for a while. Soon, a lady came in and I asked her if I could have a pilgrim dinner. She cooked up some chicken, rice, and zucchini. That was perfect for me.

A small lovely woman came in and asked if she could sit with me. She was an American from Virginia. We talked for a while. I ate and she waited for her food to be prepared. I told her I had gotten sick because I couldn't sleep with all the snorers. She told me about her earplugs that kept her from hearing anything. I was amazed. I told her about mine, which were worthless. She said she got hers at a Walgreens near her home. She searched through her bag and got me two of them. She said they hadn't been used. She could tell. I wondered how she could tell. I didn't care. I hoped they would work. She told me I would have to practice for a while before I perfected the technique. She licked her finger, took the earplug between her pointer finger and thumb, and rolled it till it was skinny. Then she put it in her ear and held it in place as it expanded, completely blocking the ear canal. I was excited to try it out. When her food came, she only ate a few bites. The chef came over and told her to eat more. She tried and ended up asking the chef to save it for her for later. When I paid, I gave the chef one of the heart rocks that I found on the Camino. She smiled and loved it. That night I tried the earplugs. They fell out twice but I got them to stay in on the third try.

I said goodbye to Trabadelo. There was a whimsical mural on a wall of fantasy figures painted in black and walking. They looked quite mythical and strangely lovely. I started out walking on the freeway, then up through a town. There was a blue Camino sign surrounded with pink flowers and red poppies with an arrow pointing up and to the left. Ugh, more uphill.

I was seeing lots of yellow arrows, one painted and faded on the street, one on a cement marker under a regular traffic sign. I walked through farmland with a farmhouse and barn surrounded by fields of green. I was glad to see more and more markers. I walked on a bridge across a river that was crystal clear except for the waterfall that was milky white. Hills of trees and hills of flowers towered above the river. Up I went into a forest of pine type trees covered with lichens and moss with ferns growing up from below. The trail got shadier and winding. I loved that it felt covered with coolness.

There was still so much uphill, but it was shady. The trail was narrow and steep, winding, and treacherous. Trees grew above the trail, shading it from the Sun until they didn't. I was grateful when they did. I was feeling like a short-timer when I saw a marker that said 187km to go to Santiago. It seemed like the uphill was a way to work off my sins. I'm sure I got dehydrated walking up the hill to La Faba. I was drinking a lot but I was sweating so much, my clothes got wet. I tied a bandana around my head to stop the sweat from going into my eyes. At the top of the hill, I sat down and rested. I just couldn't go any farther. Pilgrims walked by me. There was so much camaraderie because we were all struggling to get up the mountain together. One man came back and told me that the albergue was just around the corner. I didn't care, I couldn't move. Then I thought I'd better get there before it was full for the night and I would have to keep walking. The Albergue La Faba was surrounded by a garden with a beautiful yellow rose bush, lots of trees and plants, and a bronze sculpture of a very tired looking, walking pilgrim. A lady was sitting outside in the garden at a table checking in pilgrims. She seemed grumpy. She had a pitcher of refreshing cucumber and lemon water for us. I gave her my passport and credential, and my euros, and she gave me my stamp. She told us that there would be no pilgrim blessing at the church that night because the priest had to go to another town. I found my lower bunk, rested, and drank a lot of water.

I went out to find the mercado. I was wondering how far I would have to go. I was low on energy. I walked through the little town, past some businesses, a car repair shop, and a closed restaurant. I found the mercado. There were limited fresh vegetables. I looked for a long time before I decided what to get. I got a tomato, an onion, a couple of really awful little apples, a couple of small potatoes, and a can of pollo. I got some frozen vegetables and ice cream on a stick. By the time I figured out what I wanted, the man behind the counter was looking to close up and go home. He had a few eggs in a basket on the counter. I got them too.

I ate my ice cream on the way back to the kitchen at La Faba. I grabbed a pot and a bowl and started to prepare my food. I went to crack my egg into the bowl and with one crack it slipped out of the shell and onto the floor. I couldn't believe it. So, I had one egg for dinner with my veggies. The grumpy lady that checked us in came into the kitchen and, in drill sergeant style, said that she expected us all to do our dishes and clean up after ourselves. I sat down to eat at a table with a group of pilgrims. We talked about home, the three-day hike up the mountain, and what was to come tomorrow. When I was done eating, I noticed that there was hardly anyone left in the kitchen. There were a lot of dirty dishes and gobs of food in the sink. I thought that maybe some people didn't understand English. I trashed the food and started washing dishes. I got them all done pretty fast and sat down again. When the woman came in, I knew she was ready to yell at us for not doing the dishes. She just looked around and left. I was pleased.

I took my shower and got ready for bed. I was feeling pretty punk. I put my earplugs in and my beanie over my head and down over my eyes. I was asleep.

In the morning I made my breakfast with my other eggs and the rest of the veggies. I nuked my little potatoes, wrapped them in my bandana, and put together my stuff. Another woman and I seemed to be trying to be the last ones out. She won. My friend, Judy, had been telling me to be on the lookout for round houses with peaked roofs. I saw my first one near La Faba. It was small and behind a house. I thought maybe they used it to store fodder for the animals or it may have some other kind of storage. The land stretched out before us because we were up so high. I walked by cattle in a mountainside field. There were so many cowbells clanging, I didn't know how the cows could stand being there with all of that noise all day long. I took a panoramic video of the breathtaking view because a single picture or a series of pictures wouldn't do it justice. Pretty soon we were in the trees again.

CHAPTER 18

THE YOUNG CATHOLIC

630 KM

A young American man fell into pace with me and we started to talk. He asked me why I was on the Camino and I told him my story about my husband's illness and death. He asked me if I were Catholic. I said yes. He told me that he had been a Catholic all of his life and he was having doubts about his religion because there was so much hypocrisy and scandal. He didn't know if he wanted to be associated with the church anymore. He was on the Camino to discern his relationship with the church.

I told him about my children. I told him that I sent my children to Catholic schools all the way through high school and my heart was broken because none of them had continued in the Church. I told him that I felt so lonely in my faith but that I loved my faith and I loved my children. My home with my parents and siblings was troubled. I knew my parents loved God and they loved me, but they were acting out their pain. In my childhood, the Church was my safe place, so I loved it. I told him about a discussion I had with my son. My son told me some things his teachers told him that he couldn't agree with, like, you had to be Catholic to get into heaven. I thought that if I had heard that, I wouldn't believe it. I didn't know anyone who thought that. His teacher obviously had it wrong. I always assumed that God was bigger than religion and God was in charge of people getting into heaven. I always thought that if someone were talking about God and they weren't talking about love, mercy, and forgiveness, then they weren't really talking about God. I told my son that he was the future of the church. If he went away from the church, who was going to make it better? I told him he needed to be the one to bring about change in the church. If he went away, it was a big cop-out. I told him that he was the church and the larger church needed his clear thinking.

We arrived at the chapel at O Cebreiro. We walked in together. I went to the front to say my rosary. He knelt down closer to the back. The church seemed ancient with old rock defining the arched ceiling and the same old rock on the back wall. The roofline was uneven on one side. The other walls and ceiling looked like white thick plaster. The windows let in light that made two shadows of the large central cross one on each side of it. The atmosphere was light and sacred. There was a beautiful Medieval Virgin and Child to the side. They had a heart made out of large red roses at their feet. When I went to leave the young man had already gone.

It was a good thing that I was alone now because I needed to find some bushes. I found some really good bushes down a path across the trail from the church. There was a lot of toilet paper around on the ground. When I was done, I put my paper in my zip bag, of course.

Back on the trail, there was a bronze map of the

Camino Frances. It had an inscription on it in Spanish. The first letter of each line spelled out **CAMINOS** vertically:

Cuando el romero alcanza

A divisar el Pueblo

Mistica está su alma

Ingrávido tu cuerpo

Nota a Dios cercano

Olvida ser extraño

Sueña un bello sueño.

This is the beautiful translation, it's a bit odd but you'll get the gist:

When the pilgrim reaches

To see the town

Mystified is his soul

Weightless his body

Note to God inside,

Forget you are strange

Dream a beautiful dream.

There was also a mystical serene-looking sculpture out on a rock of a woman in greened bronze who seemed to be gazing out at the mountains. She had a bunch of green branches that someone laid on her lap between her arms. Her folded hands lay peacefully on her knees. The town was lovely and idyllic. Some of the houses were round with thatched roofs. The street was stone. Wooden markers defined its edge. There was a bar with chairs and tables outside. I wished I'd seen it before I used the bushes.

I walked quite a while without seeing any arrows. The trail was covered with brown liquid loose cow poo. The cattle were obviously having the same problem that I was. Narrowing, the trail went way down into a valley with fields on both sides. I was confused because I read it was supposed to be an easy walking day. There were goats and sheep on one side of the trail and cattle on the other. Down, down, down I went. I met a couple coming up the trail. He was from Ireland and she was from Germany They said they had gone the wrong way and I should turn around too. Oh my, I just turned an easy day into a hard day. I was thankful they saved me from going even farther down. We climbed back up. At the town, he found the yellow arrow we missed and directed me to follow them. We all marveled at how we had missed that arrow. I didn't see it. I was looking for an arrow and I didn't find one. Sometimes the arrows were far apart and I had to just keep walking forward, hoping to see one soon. The young couple powered on ahead of me.

On the trail again, at the start of Galicia, there was a large asymmetrical low rounded hut with a high thatched roof with a spiral at the tip-top. Seemed like the floor must have been lower inside or something. The walls were short and made out of stone. There was a doorway in the tallest part of the wall. I would have to get on my knees to go in there. There were trees all around.

The dirt trail started going up through mostly chaparral with a few slender trees to the sides. Deeper into a shady wood, flowers dotted the mossy hillside. Little white ones and tall yellow dandelions seemed bright against the deep green undergrowth. I was surrounded now with pine trees and trees with flowers that looked like pale pink apple blossoms. A wooden fence along the trail protected a culvert. Some little yellow flowers looked shiny as if they were made out of patent leather. They were surrounded by young, spring green fern sprouts. Further on, little pink flowers shot up tall out of clumps of grass. A splendid array of blue, white, and yellow tiny flowers looked lush with natural mulch and twisted branches around. Larger leaves were the backdrop for tiny white flowers with long stamens that made them look like fairies dancing among blue little flowers with white centers. It reminded me of "The Forest Primeval" in the book *Evangeline* by Henry Wadsworth Longfellow. The trail started going down and a sheer rocky cliff gave way to a steep grassy mountainside that smoothly stretched down to civilization far below. As always, I was glad to see a yellow arrow painted on a cement block wall urging me on and letting me know I wasn't lost. I was delighted to see banks of holly bushes with cheery red berries. Through the trees, I could see a paved road below.

Walking down the road, I came to Fonfría. Samir had recommended it as a place for my birthday, but since I was sick, I didn't make it there by then. He said they throw a party for dinner and it would be fun. I was excited to participate now. A party sounded really good! I signed in at the bar and got my bunk and dinner. I found a lower bunk against a wall of curtains that separated the bunk room from the entryway. I went back to the bar and got a cerveza con limon, an agua grande, and four fruit popsicles. At my bunk again, I unloaded my pack of all the things I would need, placing them under my bunk. I pulled out my sleeping bag and took a rest. An interesting older man was in the lower bunk next to mine. He was Jewish and from New York. He had traveled the Camino before. He said he always made sure he stopped at Fonfría for a good time. Across the room, I saw an older couple whom I had seen at another albergue. They waved to me in recognition.

At the appointed time, I went to the dining hall down the hill behind the bar. It was an older building made from stone. When I walked in a young man told me I was too early. Then a lady came by and said, "No, let them in; its time." Inside, there were two levels. The kitchen was on the first level with stairs going up to the dining area. Long tables were around the edges, two rows deep. I sat down at a table against the wall. The tables were set with baskets of bread, bottles of water and wine, plates, and silverware. Pilgrims arrived, filtering in slowly, old and young alike. Pretty soon, the place was noisy with talking. The man next to me was from Russia. He looked sad. He spoke English rather well. His daughter lived in England with her mother and he missed her so much. He said that everything he did was for her. He worked and sent money to them. His wife wouldn't let him see his daughter, even though she was all grown up now. I told him he should meet her on the Camino and they could walk the Camino together. He smiled and nodded and said, "Maybe we will." After dinner, the music whipped up from dining music to dancing music. The owner came out and told us we were going to have a good time dancing. She found a dance partner and invited everyone to dance. Lots of people were dancing. About the second song, I asked the guy from Russia if he liked to dance. He said, "Yes." Then he looked at me and asked me if I wanted to dance. I nodded and we went to the dance floor and danced. After one dance, he said he had to leave. I think he was going to cry. I tried dancing by myself for a while. I love to dance so much. I found some ladies who were dancing and I just acted like I was dancing with them too. Everyone was having fun.

I didn't stay long at the dance. I went back to my bunk and slept. In the morning, I packed up and got breakfast at the bar. I think that the same lady was waiting for me to leave so she could be the last one there again. I asked the guy at the bar which way to go to Santiago. He pointed down the road. There was supposed to be no uphill that day, just lovely rolling hills. I saw a yellow arrow and a trail leading off the road and up into farm country.

Walking on, I came to a grassy area that looked over a wide valley of farmland. The view seemed like it was of a mysterious far off land misty and blue in the distance. The trail went into a valley. It was a bit overgrown with greenery, with dirt showing through in two lines, tire track distance apart. One farmer had taken large sheets of slate and stood them up to make his fence, another created a piled-up fieldstone rock wall.

I came to a little town with a bar and an outside dining area. I got a café Americano and went to the restroom. The barman brought my café out to me on the patio. I sat under an umbrella, took my boots off, put my feet up on a chair, and leaned back to rest. By the time I was ready to leave, I had to go again. I was starting to be concerned about my urinary tract health. I got back on the road. A round stone building with a thatched roof had a happy blue Camino sign with a yellow shell and arrow. It also had two painted yellow arrows on it. I walked through the countryside with farms as far as I could see. I saw a hand-made sign and stopped into a coffee shop in a lady's backyard. I got a café and a frozen fruit bar and gratefully used the restroom.

CHAPTER 19

TRIACASTELA

645 KM

After a day of walking, I got to Triacastela. I went to the bar in town, Pension Residencia Garcia, to use their facilities. It was a bar, restaurant, and hotel. There were a lot of tables and chairs outside as well as inside. I went inside and got a serving of tortilla and showed them the address of my albergue. The man took me outside and pointed back down the road to Xunta. I also asked him where a farmacia was. He pointed in the other direction and said, "In town. Take the road to the right." So, I went to my albergue. When I arrived, the lady said they were full. I told her I had a reservation. She looked my name up on her list. She told me to come back later when she would be doing the sign in.

I went into town and found the pharmacy. It was a long walk. The street forked and went in two directions. I took the high road to the right. I walked by well-maintained houses and businesses on the outskirts. The pharmacy was way at the far end of town. I noticed a couple of mercados that I passed along the way. After I consulted with the pharmacy lady, she told me to eat bananas and rice and no milk products. She gave me another medication for urinary tract infection, a medication for diarrhea, another cough meds, electrolytes, probiotics, and Advil for my inflamed ankle. It seemed like I had the entire pharmacy in my bag. I went to the grocery store and got some bananas, rice cakes, apples, and two agua grandes. I was looking for some pectin candy or fruit roll without sugar. I didn't find it so I got some little jam squares.

I hiked back to my albergue. I got in line to sign in. The lady found my name again, took my information, and gave me my stamp. I found a lower bunk and laid down on my sleeping bag. I put my heart rocks that I found that day in a row on the table by my bed. I found that if I put them in a row, they helped each other look more like hearts. Some of them were a bit misshaped. The lady in the bunk next to mine commented that I was very neat and organized. I gave her one of the heart rocks. I usually tried to give most of them away each day.

I went down to the laundry. There was a line to get a washer. I asked a lady if I could do laundry with her. She said she had a lot with her two companions, so I waited. Some women came in after me. They had bags of laundry. I was glad I wasn't behind them in line. I hung my clothes out on my clothesline because their clotheslines were full. I hung mine between two trees on the side of the albergue. It was a bit perilous because the ground was uneven and the limb on the tree was quite high. I was very careful.

I went up to the bar to get dinner. I got rice and chicken and salad for dinner. I sat outside on the patio. A lot of pilgrims were enjoying their food together with lots of wine being drunk. I got a glass. I enjoyed my dinner as long as I could. I went back to the albergue and went to sleep. I wish I had known the ladies' bathroom was downstairs. I had to go down there several times during the night. The next day I wasn't feeling very well. I told the albergue mama and she said I could stay another night. I got a bunk downstairs the next night.

I tried to leave after the second day. I had to pee at 3 bars walking through town. I got to the bottom of the hill near the pharmacy and had to pee again. I found a bush but had to pee again really fast. I figured I wouldn't be able to walk that day. The pharmacy lady sold me another bottle of pills: a "natural antibiotic" and she told me to go to a hotel. She called ahead and found me one. I went to the hotel and the lady gave me the address of her friend's other hotel. I went in there. I stayed there for two nights, sleeping, drinking and peeing. I found a restaurant in town that had a big bowl of soup with chicken, broth, cabbage, onions, and potatoes. I went there for lunch and dinner on both days. It had an indoor and outdoor dining room. The outdoor tables were covered with red and white checkered oilcloth. The people who ate there were from the town, not pilgrims. Many didn't seem to be Spanish.

I felt better after the two additional days, or four days in all, in Triacastela. I felt confident to walk on. I got my stuff together and checked out of the hotel. I had my pack transported to San Mamede. The walk was lovely out of town; I was in a primeval forest again. I walked over a wooden bridge that had a rushing river below. There were little pink flowers on the bank among the bushes and ferns. It made me want to stand there and daydream a while. Soon, I was on a paved road again, past a green hill and trees under a blue sky smattered with puffy clouds. The layers of ferns against the grass and a forest silhouetted against the clouds and the wide blue sky were breathtaking. I started seeing purple foxglove along the trail. Plants and vines were bright green as I walked on a switchback trail following the many signs. What a wonderful day of sauntering. I stopped into many small churches that were open. A churchyard had many aboveground crypts with crosses on each and statues of the virgin. I walked in a forest of oak trees covered with lichens, ferns, and vines. I would like to have gone to an art shop that had some lovely signs along the way; but it was some distance from the trail and I was feeling like I didn't have any extra energy, so I kept following the yellow arrows.

I got to San Mamede and walked in on the wide shiny black-tiled walkway. The garden was extensive, with tables and chairs on the grass and many flower beds. The owner's daughter took me into her office and signed me in. It was bunk and dinner for one price, as no restaurants were close by. She led me to a room with five bunk beds. I chose the lower bunk by the bathroom. I laid down and rested. Later, I gave her my euros and my laundry, which she washed and I took my clothes and hung them in the garden. I was grateful to buy an agua grande from the owner. He said I was lucky he had an extra that day. I really enjoyed interacting with the people at San Mamede. An older guy, Stan, from Germany, was quite philosophical. He seemed to be amused and wise about many things.

Dinner was lentil soup, Spanish omelet, cake, and fruit. During dinner, the owner told the group the history of San Mamede. A large and ancient picture of a family hung on the wall. It had a beautiful curvy wooden frame and the family was dressed in their Sunday best. They were the previous owners. He also told us that his family wanted to sell the albergue because he and his wife were getting too old to take care of it. His daughter was helping him do the work until it was sold.

I was feeling very poorly. I went into the kitchen and asked one of the kitchen staff, who spoke English, how I could get to see a doctor. He said that he lived in town and he would take me to the medical center 15 minutes away, on the way home, after he did the dishes. The owner told him to take me and he would do the dishes. I must have looked pretty bad. He drove me to the medical center. He took me in and made sure the medical staff knew why I was there. The nurse gave me the bottle to pee in and did the urinalysis. They took a bunch of information from me, looked at my passport, and my medical insurance cards. I waited on a bench. She called me in to see the doctor. He said I had an infection. He wrote me a prescription. There was no charge. I assumed the clinic took my insurance information and would contact the insurance company. He told me to walk down the street to the pharmacy and get the medication. I walked down there and it was closed. He was watching me and could see, when I turned around and came back, that the pharmacy was closed. He walked down the street and met me. He took me to the taxi lane. He told the cab driver where the all-night pharmacy was, to take me there and wait for me and then take me back to the Albergue San Mamede. I got the medication. It was 5 euros. Not worth bothering my insurance about, and I didn't want to carry the receipt. When I got back to the albergue, I paid the driver the 10 euros he asked for. The whole thing took about an hour. I went to my bunk to read the directions and take my meds. It said to put the powder in a glass of water and drink it, and to do the same with the other packet 24 hours later. Okay, that was easy. I took the meds and went to bed.

In the middle of the night, I woke up and noticed that poop and pee were coming out of me without my permission! WHAT??? I jumped up out of my sleeping bag and ran into the bathroom without my flashlight. I sat down and tried to decide what to do. My sleep sack nightie was soiled! It was a coed bathroom so I couldn't just go out into the bathroom without my nightie on. I tried to get it off over my head without getting it in my hair. I stood up, flushed, washed the back of my nightie out in the toilet in the dark, and dried it a bit with paper. I put it on and went into the shower and cleaned off the rest of me. I went back to bed but had to get up a couple of more times. Ugh! I took my diarrhea meds. I was glad that my nightie was made out of negative ion fabric that wicks water out and it dries fast.

The next morning, I was feeling a little better but I was still tied to the bathroom. I went into the dining room. There were still a few pilgrims toasting bread and applying butter and jam. Stan from Germany was lamenting about the lack of Nutella. There was cocoa mix to make hot chocolate. I got some coffee. There was a little tortilla left from dinner. I ate that. Stan spread his toast thick with butter, sprinkled cocoa mix over it, and gave it a smear and said, "Ah, Nutella." We all laughed. I had my pack transported to Morgade, my next stop.

I got on the road but I had to find bushes all along the road into Sarria. I was getting really good at not being self-conscious about my bodily functions. I wanted to go into Sarria and go to the medical center and get a different medication, one that didn't give me the trots. I found the medical center by asking people on the street. I went in and asked to see someone about the meds. They scrambled to find someone who spoke English. I was told to go upstairs and I would see a doctor. They gave me the room number. I went up and used the restroom and then I looked for the room number. I went in. That was the wrong thing to do. She told me to wait in the lobby. I waited. She called me in. I showed her my meds and she said that medication was known to cause diarrhea. Wow! That really made me mad. What kind of human being gives a woman, who they know is sleeping in a sleeping bag, meds that cause diarrhea without telling her about it? So, the doctor thought that he would cure me of one problem by causing another problem. I couldn't believe it. She told me that she couldn't give me another medication until that one took its course. I told her that I still hurt down there. She said I would be better soon. I told her I was afraid to take the second dose. She told me not to take it. She thought one dose should cure me. She had me lay on an examination table and she examined my belly. Then she told me to rest in Sarria for three days before I continued. I told her I didn't have time to wait three days. I had already taken so many sick days off. I couldn't wait to get out of there.

Out on the street, I asked some people where the Camino was. They didn't know. I asked a lady in a shop and she pointed to the river and said to follow the river and I would see the yellow arrows. I walked down along the grassy bank of the river until I saw an arrow up on a sidewalk, I was back on the road to Santiago.

CHAPTER 20

ONE WEEK AND 100 KM TO GO

664 KM

Walking out of Sarria was just what I wanted to do! The sidewalk had a shell motif down the center every few feet. There were yellow arrows painted right on the sidewalk. The people of Galicia provide a lot of yellow arrow signs for the pilgrims. That is good because at that point, the weary don't need the added stress of getting lost. There was an iron fence with giant iron shells along a walkway with beautiful trees and bushes on the other side. Green makes everything better. I walked by a tall wall mural of a gigantic white-bearded pilgrim and other smaller pilgrims walking the Camino. It said, "Zapatones, 1954-2015." The wall had a copious number of vines growing over the top at just the right spot to make it look like Zapatones had a big green Afro hair style.

The sidewalk turned into a path and into a trail along a road past yellow and green flowering fields. I saw another white horse in a field with his friends, the brown cattle. Trees were all around. An arrow painted on a rock in a field let me know I was going the right way. There were so many arrows it seemed like they were celebrating our presence there. Dark clouds were rolling in thicker and thicker. The contrast of the trees on the dark grey sky was striking. I walked by a mysterious oak forest with branches that looked like they were dancing with vines growing up the trees and ferns down below. I was looking for twisted trees, but there were none. In San Diego, we have a lot of twisted trees. Someone told me that the spirits came up from the nether world through twisted trees. I guessed the Spanish spirits were staying put. I walked down a beautiful trail that had oak trees on each side. They grew at each other above and created a leafy Cathedral-like canopy to walk under. The trees were dappled with moss and lichens. I noticed little purple columbines nestled against a rock surrounded by ferns, baby oak sprouts and berry vines. A little robin with a red breast in a tree watched me walk by. More cattle grazed in a field, this time black and white; along with all white ones. I saw a curious tree that looked like it had fig leaves but it had little black berries. Maybe they were elderberries? I walked along a moss encrusted rock wall with ivy growing over it until I got to an ancient stone building that was part of the wall. It was attached to a large stone house under tall trees and ivy was growing up the building. Rolling hills covered with green reminded me of Ireland. Next, I saw a furrowed dirt field with baby corn sprouts just looking up and then another forest primeval with ferns dancing up out of the mulchy earth. The purple foxgloves were plentiful.

When I came into Casa Morgade Hotel, it was raining. The bar was inviting and warm with lots of dark wood on the walls and the furniture. Sitting down to rest, I got a café Americana, no more leche for me! The check in was at the bar. I asked if there were laundry services, and the man said no. My room was at the top of the stairs. It was charming with pure white walls and dark wood floor, ceiling, and furniture. The bathroom was down the hall. It had a beautiful ceramic sink with a bright blue and yellow sunflower design. Out the window of my room, I noticed that the weather had cleared. I saw a patio in the back of the hotel. I went out to sit in the Sun. I met some women who were out sunning too. They invited me to eat dinner with them later. Though I may have been the oldest one, no one was young. I got a salad and they shared a sausage and cheese plate. One woman was excited to try a special local dish that had something to do with cheese. She also ordered some aperitif to share, in three flavors, one was local. They were brought to us after dinner, on a plate, a collection of tiny glasses. They were delightful. We talked about many things. I met a lady from England who helped me with transportation savvy when I was finding my way home. One woman mentioned that if you don't walk the whole Camino, you have to get two stamps a day from Sarria to the end. I was glad I didn't have to worry about that, but that information was wrong. I found out later in Santiago, when I was getting my compastela, that I should have gotten the two stamps even though I walked the whole way. They made an exception and gave it to me anyway, but the manager had to be consulted. I told everyone to look around because we were all strong powerful women who were willing to do what it took to walk the Camino Santiago de Compostela. We made a toast to us all.

Bedtime was decision time. I had been considering if I should take the second dose of the medication. I didn't want to have the same reaction as before. I wanted to sleep in the night so I didn't want to be up in the bathroom all night like before. I wasn't feeling good still. I didn't want the sickness to stay with me. I wanted to stamp it out. I went back and forth. I had to take it by 10 pm because that was 24 hours. In the end I drank the "Kool-Aid" closer to 11:00 pm and took two anti-diarrhea pills with it. I said my great prayer, "Dear God, please make everything turn out okay." I couldn't wait for everything to turn out okay. In the stillness of the night I heard loud snoring in another room. Augh, I would have to wear my ear plugs tonight as well. I did sleep most of the night, aside from getting up to go 6 times.

The next morning, I got breakfast at the inn and was on my way to find bars to use the restroom as the day progressed. I was walking only about 10 km a day in my compromised health condition. The towns were only about 2 km apart in that part of Galicia.

After a day of walking through beautiful countryside, I came to a town, Gonzar. It was dry, dirty, and desolate. The buildings were old bare wood or hadn't been painted for a long time, the colors were dark brown, black, and brown. No one was around. Walking through the streets gave me the creeps. I started to have second thoughts about staying there. When I got to the albergue, all of my fears vanished. The place was lively. It was a rambling establishment with happy people at a great bar and a patio in the center with a bunk house, dining room, and conference room around it. I signed in with the young lady at the bar. She told me that if I had laundry to do, she would do it for me. I was glad to get my sleep sack nighty washed in a machine with real soap. The bunk house was long and had two rooms. A church group took over the second bunk room and the conference room.

I settled into my bunk, gathered my laundry, and took it to the bar. The nice lady took it and some euros from me and left with it. I came back later and asked her if it was done because I wanted to hang it up. She said that she had already hung it up. Wow, I thanked her and went to have lunch in the dining room. On the table, my plate with eggs, ham and salad; a black cup of coffee; cruets with oil and vinegar; and a glass of water were accompanied by my pile of pills; two bottles, one with my probiotic and the other with my electrolytes; eating utensils; and napkin. Soon after I was done eating, the bar lady came and told me I'd better get my clothes off the line because it was starting to rain. I asked her where they were. She pointed out the gate and down the street. I really didn't want to go out there, but I did. I walked down the street. The clothesline was out in a field. I gathered my clothes while it sprinkled on me. I was amazed the clothes were dry. The wind on the Camino was great for drying clothes.

I had dinner in the dining room with some other women. One of the ladies was there the night before. I mentioned that the previous night at Morgade, I heard a snorer who snored so loudly that I had to wear my earplugs in my private room! She said, "That would be me." She said that she invited another woman to share her room that night but she left before dawn. I thought, *Wow, that poor woman probably couldn't sleep all night and she thought she might as well walk as to lay there and not sleep.* I was so grateful for that woman who gave me her ear plugs. The snorer got animated and told me "What's the big deal? People should get over it. People snore." I told her that I could see her point but I was sick because my resistance was down from not sleeping five nights in a row. She got unanimated and quiet. The entertainment at dinner wafted in from the conference room where the church group was having their dinner and an achievement ceremony. Their singing was lively and festive. They told jokes in their language and the laughing was merry. I noticed that the bar woman was in the kitchen preparing the dinner too. I imagined that the establishment was a family operation.

At bed time, I waited in line for the bathroom behind the group. One of the counselors told them to let me ahead of the line. That was nice. When I woke up in the morning the snorer was gone already.

When I left, I noticed some pilgrim art on a rock wall. There was a Knights Templars cross and a silly stylized picture of a pilgrim with a blue bunny head and a staff and gourd with a triangular red dress and yellow feet walking. Below the figure was a yellow arrow pointing the way. Along the wall were benches for pilgrims to rest.

That day, while walking, I had to stop many times. When I went into a bar, I had to buy something so I could use their bathroom. Coffee at the first place, tortilla next, apricot juice next, agua grande next, cerveza con limon next, and the final place I was hungry but they didn't have anything I could eat, so I got a coffee. The walk was great, sauntering first through farmland. I saw black and white cattle in a field. One cow had her head over a fence eating the plants on the other side. She was so cute, coyly looking up at me over the fence as I walked by with her pink and black nose and her number tag jewelry in her ear. The path became stone slabs above a stream rolling down a rock drain along a lush green meadow. Oak trees dotted the landscape. This is where I started seeing black slugs on the trail. I walked by a small old stone church with a slate roof. Part of the church was made out of squared off stones and the other part was out of many sizes of curved stone, like maybe it was an older part of the church. It had two bell towers and a cool horreo outside that looked like a castle. Horreos were small huts used to store grain. They were set up on pillars to discourage rodents.

I came to the 100 km to go marker. It was decorated with graffiti and a crowd of people had gathered around it taking pictures. A young woman came rushing up and told people to step aside because, "I own this." After she had someone take her picture, I asked her why she said she owned it. She said that she had walked all the way from St. Jean and she deserved it. I told her that I walked from St. Jean too. She looked surprised. A lot of people start the Camino in Sarria. It's the last place you can start and still get the Compostela certificate when you get to Santiago. I guess she thought that most of the people there were just starting. She may have been right. I had someone take my picture in front of the marker too. It had a yellow shell on a dark blue tile above a yellow arrow with Km. 100,000 below that. I guess they use a comma instead of a period. The marker readings from there on were very precise to the third decimal. The young woman, "who owned the marker," came up to me on the trail and asked me when I started the Camino at St. Jean. I told her I started on April 5 and had been walking for almost 2 months. She said she thought that was great. Smile...

I appreciated the interesting and creative fences made out of bits and pieces of different materials. One rock wall incorporated a tall pointed stone slab, and it was held up by a rusty metal strap looped around an ancient wooden pole. It had a metal bracket attached lower on the pole which continued the fence with a metal frame filled in with small chain link. It was all covered in moss of green, some lumpy and mottled, some smooth like a blanket; and the tall stone had a patina of orange. The back drop was an oak forest with reaching branches and ferns poking out of the lush green undergrowth. As it started raining I passed an ancient rock wall that was completed with stucco into a building with a slanted roof. It was painted with huge two-toned green leaves, with little oranges and bananas flying around. I loved the whimsical art. As the road wound gently before me, I could see people in the distance and didn't feel alone. Another interesting fence came into view that was made with old wooden farm equipment turned on its side and completed with regular fence lumber. Ancient villages were accentuated with modern vehicles that seemed out of place. Walking along was like taking a walk through my old jewelry box. So many treasures from the past at every turn. A cement cross here, a row of flowered bushes there, all of it hugging the ground which marked the Holy Way of St. James.

I came to a lake. There was a colorful array of people on the black top paved path, some with walking sticks and some without. Everyone had a backpack, some had hats, some not. The lake was surrounded by a silhouette of trees of different varieties and colors of green. Some were rounded, some pointy and some tall. Hills of dark green chaparral and then a hilltop farm of light green fields were in the distance with the serene dark blue lake nestled in the valley. The town of Portomarín was a series of homes and buildings that seemed to be climbing up another green hill. I walked down the paved road until the arrows led to a dirt and rocky trail. It was steep and it seemed to have steps for giants that were as tall as my legs. I had to navigate from one to the next. People started helping me by taking my arm to guide me. A man went before me and pushed the small rocks away before I put my foot down. It was a totally surreal experience to be fussed over like that. I was wondering if it were because I was old or if I looked that sick. Probably both. Maybe they were God's angels.

I wanted to go into Portomarín but I was feeling so punk that I couldn't think of climbing up the giant staircase that led up to the town. I knew I had to keep going if I was going to make it to Palais del Rey. I walked on and was looking for a bush to do my business. Seeing no bush, in desperation I went behind someone's dumpster right before it was too late. They drove into their driveway as I was finishing up. I prayed for rain to wash it away and followed an arrow out into the wilderness. The hills seemed to comfort me as the trees came together up above me on the dirt trail littered with leaves, ferns tickled out to soften my edges, and a pooled stream stood still in the quiet.

Pretty soon I was in farmland again. The wide dirt

trail was edged on each side with tall sparse conifers, and the field came right up to the trail. I passed a row of large cylinders of hay that were about 4 feet tall and 4 feet long and coated with black or white plastic. The blue sky was punched with cumulous clouds at the tree-lined far horizon. Further on, the deep green colors of the farm land were enriched by dark brown dirt fields and dark green trees and bushes. I noticed that the yellow flowered bushes were developing into bushes of silvery fuzzy spirals. It was exciting to think that I had been there so long that I witnessed the cycle of the flowers to seed pods.

I met a man from the United States who was walking alone. He was a missionary in South Korea working with the youth. We started talking about many things. He said he was on the Camino to figure out what was God's will for him. I told him that God was waiting around to find out what he wanted to do so God could will it. I told him that God had given us free will, so it was up to him to engage in his life, develop his desires, and go after them. That was how God created. He created using our genius and our noticing what would please us. It was sort of a cop out for him to shove it back to God and not take responsibility for engaging in his life to find out what delighted him. He agreed with me but said that you can't just tell people that. I said, "Well, I think you had better tell people that or they won't realize their potential and the world won't be as outrageously spectacular if people don't go after the wonderfulness that exists for them." Then he told me that I should write a book. I said, who would read it? He said that he would read it. His phone rang. Another person in his group was wondering where he was. He had brought a group of young people to the Camino. He started walking faster to catch up with them and left me behind.

I came to an industrial looking farm operation with large low buildings and what seemed like a sea of silos. It seemed dry and blighted. I hoped I would find a town with a bar near, but not yet. A sign with a pilgrim and an arrow pointed out into a tree lined trail up a hill. I walked and walked. I passed a beagle that seemed to know where he was going. The country got soft with rounded bushes and tall grass. A tree with yellow flowers that looked like apple blossoms delighted me and little yellow and white daisies and purple thistle-like clovers waved at me close to the ground. How lovely! A canopy of trees stretched out and seemed to create a soft expansive room that the trail led me through. Around a bend an anomaly presented itself. It was like a living room with many couches and coffee tables right under the trees. It had a trailer with a kitchen set up next to it. I could see a man in the kitchen. I walked up and noticed that he was frying two well done hamburgers. There was a menu. I asked him if I could have a hamburger and a café. He went into the trailer and brought back the hamburger and put it on to fry. I wanted to sit down and be in the living room for a while. I asked if he had a restroom. He said, "No, but there will be more bushes soon." When the hamburger was ready, I decided to eat it while I walked so I could get to my albergue as soon as possible. As I walked away, I noticed a smiling woman watching me. She was lazing in a hammock strung between two trees.

A Km 85,924 marker post sported two blue tiles, one with a yellow shell and the other with a yellow arrow. It was topped with a large piece of bark that held maybe 10 large pinecones. Many little rocks and sticks were also balanced on it. The all-lower-case word "galicia" was written at the bottom of the post, fun.

CHAPTER 21

PALAIS DEL REY

710 KM

I came to another farm in the distance. It was greener and smaller than the previous one. The path led down a hill into Palais del Rey, a town built on hills. I felt like I was walking through a children's book of charming blocks of businesses connected by very wide cement streets that seemed to pour down the hillsides into each other. I asked someone where my albergue was by showing them the address in my book. They pointed down a street. I kept asking people until I came to a rural road that seemed like it went nowhere. I got to the bottom of the hill and noticed the sign for the albergue. I walked in. A man was checking pilgrims in at the dining room table. He pointed to a bin by the door where I deposited my hiking sticks. I got my bunk and dinner; breakfast would be on the road. The man took me upstairs while he told me the rules. In the morning the door would be locked and after we left we couldn't get back in. We should make sure we took all our stuff because he wouldn't be back until the next afternoon. I was surprised and glad when I heard him say, "No smoking." He let me choose a bunk. I got the lower one right across from the bathroom. It ended up I was the only woman in the bunk room that night. My bunk mates were a minister and his friend, a man from Russia, and a man from the Netherlands. A private room downstairs housed a couple. I laid down for a rest after hitting the bathroom. While I was resting, I smelled some marijuana smoke from the bunk in the corner. I was disappointed because it was a smoke-free environment. The man from downstairs came up to investigate. The man from Amsterdam denied that he was smoking as did everyone else.

It turned out that the man who checked us in was the chef as well. He sang and said he loved preparing our food. Dinner was pasta with seafood sauce, salad and red wine. It was delicious. In conversation, I found out that the couple was there to check out the albergues because they wanted to purchase one and live on the Camino. I told them about San Mamede. The man from Russia said he was walking the Camino Primitivo. He had a wife and child and lived in Germany. He was a financial person for the government. He spoke perfect American English. He said he spent some time in America as a teenager. He told me that it was too bad that President Trump was fighting with the countries of the world. I asked him to define fighting. He said that the United States used to give billions of dollars to other countries to pay the trade deficit. Now the US didn't do that; and so, the countries that used to get all of that free money were having to scramble to make up for the funds that they were no longer getting. I questioned if that were really fighting. He told me that Trump should have done it more slowly. I told him that Trump only had 4 years to do whatever he was going to do. The minister was quiet, and his friend was an enjoyable conversationalist. Later, he told me about the minister and that he was a very holy man. They were a church group traveling together. His wife was with another part of the group in another town.

I got a good night's sleep and before I left, the minister's friend told me that he wanted to give me a blessing. As he prayed over me, I hoped it would help me get over my illnesses.

The dirt trail left the albergue and skirted a school that was just starting their day. Classical music seemed to organize the children as they talked and laughed. A lady on a loudspeaker gave direction as a hush came over the children. I continued past and down an alley and finally saw another yellow arrow painted on a steel fence bar and pointing to the main road. I walked past little shops with cottage windows, all dark inside but cheery yellow, black, and white on the outside. Ahead, I saw an arrow pointing up an incline into a forested area. "Oh no!" I realized I forgot to bring my poles with me. They were in the bin by the door of the kitchen dining room. A man walking by me said, "What's wrong?" I told him I left my poles. My mind was racing remembering that the chef-proprietor told us the door would lock behind us, so I couldn't go back for them anyway. All of a sudden, I felt free. It was like my walking sticks were a barrier between me and the Camino and all of the people. I realized that I was glad they were gone. I told the man that I wasn't going back for them and why. He said, "Are you sure? There are some pretty big hills between here and Santiago." I told him that I was sure and we walked on together.

He talked about his Camino. He had walked the Camino many times. This time he started in Sarria and was going to do his Camino on a long weekend. He looked very trim and athletic in his running shorts and a tank top. He reminded me remarkably of my athletic husband. He told me about his home, including his wife and daughter. He didn't want to leave his wife alone taking care of their daughter for too long. He was grateful that she agreed to let him have this time to himself. He was involved in city business and in his town. He needed a respite because of the politics that made his job a strain. We spoke of our families and our lives. I was surprised that he was willing to walk slowly with me.

He told me that as a young runner, he always tried to hold his body tight so he could be strong and fast. Now he was having trouble with being winded. I told him that I was a Transformational Breathing Facilitator and about the need to breathe in his belly. He said it would be difficult because he always tried to have a hard belly when he ran. I told him about when I ran a marathon years before doing a six-step breathing pattern: breathing in for 6 steps and out for 6 steps. It got me through. I was using it on the Camino too but I did an 8-step breath, 6 steps breathing in and two steps out when the terrain was flat. When a hill came, I went to 4 in and 2 out and then 2 in and 2 out when it was really steep. I thought when it got steeper my body needed a faster turnaround of air because I had more toxins to breathe out from stress when the walking got difficult. His story about his job being stressful made sense. I shared that anxiety is made out of not enough oxygen. When we are stressed, we naturally do high-chest breathing. It is a component of the fight or flight response. When we don't get enough oxygen, our body panics. That panic feeling is the anxiety feeling.

If we consciously breathe deeply with our full lungs at times like this, our anxiety is alleviated. He seemed excited and was grateful and thanked me. He was sure it would help him. He needed to breathe more.

He asked me if I spoke Spanish. I said I took two years of Spanish in high school and one year in college and live right by Mexico in southern California, so I could get by when no one spoke English. I had even helped people in San Diego when Spanish-speaking people had trouble communicating in restaurants or other businesses that I happen to witness. Most people spoke English. He decided that he needed to do me a good turn too. So, he told me to only speak to him in Spanish. He told me that I needed practice. I was enjoying talking to him so much and trying to find the Spanish words for what I wanted to say to him was difficult. I started saying the Spanish words and put in English words when I didn't know the next Spanish word. It was so hard. He was patient and he said the words I stumbled on. I said a few English sentences, and he said, "No, say it in Spanish!" Ugh. I smiled and continued.

We walked through the forest and into a town with

houses with neatly manicured gardens. We decided to have breakfast together at the little forest restaurant, which was the only business in the town. The tables were outside. I ordered eggs and salad. He ordered toast and ham. They gave us a lot of food! He told me about the Spanish black-leg ham. He said that it's a famous delicacy. People buy a ham and keep it hanging in the kitchen for months. The men are taught to carve the ham thinly. I asked him if he knew how to carve the ham. He smiled widely and said yes. He said that it's good luck to have one of these hams. The local people say that you have a black leg when they say you have good luck. Like, when a baby is born, you have a black leg. I asked him if I should tell people they have a black leg. He said, only in northern Spain, not in Mexico. He also told me to be sure to get some octopus in Melide. I told him that I was worried that it might be tough. He said it wasn't. He asked me if I had ever eaten it. I told him I had baby octopus at a restaurant at home. They brought it with a bunch of other seafood to the table on a hibachi grill. It was tender. He said they really know how to make octopus in Melide and that I would love it. When we had eaten as much as we wanted, he said he was finished. I said I had to use the restroom. He went on ahead.

After we parted and I was walking, I realized that I no longer felt sick. I was walking with that skip in my step that I enjoyed so much. I thanked God for sending me this angel to cheer me up, body and soul.

I continued my walk to Melide, up and down hills on a dirt path surrounded by ancient oak trees, past a babbling brook that meandered under a cement walking path bridge. The foliage was lovely ferns and floating leaves tied to trees on tiny thin branches that drooped down to skim the water. Rocks were mossy green and grey. It smelled positively medicinal. I was in heaven marveling at the beauty all around me and appreciating every moment of still being there, with my short time left on the Camino. Farms with tiny seedlings on brown fields made lines in different directions. I came to a town that had a church with a rope leading up to a bell. Another pilgrim was pulling the rope but it didn't ring the bell. I loved the statue of a pilgrim in front of Casa De Los Somoza. The Camino was celebrated in so many ways. There were statues of folk figures. A man with a bagpipe and a woman with a tambourine graced a park-like setting. I came to a bridge with three arches. In the town, I discovered a bar with a smiling pilgrim sign out front next to the sign advertising all of the different ice cream possibilities. A church had a crucifix with Jesus reaching down from the cross. Walking into Melide was long. I followed the arrows. My book said that if I followed the arrows it would lead to my albergue. So, I walked through neighborhoods one block off of the main drag till it led me through town to O Cruceiro Albergue in a large official-looking building. The inside had colorful tile on the walls and floor. It had a kitchen, but no meals were provided. I went to the check-in desk and gave them my passport and credential. I was shown upstairs to a bunk room with four bunk beds. I laid out my sleeping bag and took a nap. I knew I had to go find some pulpo, or octopus, for dinner. I also knew that I would have to be very hungry to be able to eat it. I waited till I was hungry. The beds slowly filled up. One bunk bed was a father and daughter, another was an English couple whom I had seen before. The husband had ruined his foot somehow, but he didn't want to stop walking. He wasn't going to a doctor with his foot because he didn't want to be told to stop walking. The wife said that they were walking slowly the rest of the way. I admired her for being supportive of him. I couldn't believe how chivalrous the husband was. When he found out that I had left my poles behind, he offered me his. I told him that I thought he would need them more than me. I went out and found a grocery store to buy food for breakfast and lunch on the trail the next day.

I would like to have had someone to eat my pulpo with, but no one was around when I got hungry. I went out to find a restaurant that was recommended to me. I actually went down the wrong road and missed it, so I asked google maps to show me how to get there. I walked in and didn't know what to do. I watched until another group came in and ordered. I went up to the lady by the menu sign and pointed to what I thought I wanted. Then I sat down and waited. I was brought a bowl and a bottle of wine and some thick-cut white bread. I thought the wine was a good idea but I was worried about being able to drink that much. I sat next to an American lady who was there with her two brothers. She talked to me about her experience with eating the pulpo. She offered me some but it was cold and I decided to wait for mine. The waitress brought me a small wooden platter of steaming purple pulpo with suction cups on tentacles. I started to eat. It was tender. I realized that I could have gotten some hot potatoes. So, I ordered them. They helped by giving me more texture to my food, especially after the pulpo got cold. I ate until I was full. I left the smallest tendrils on the platter. I ate a bunch of crunchy sweet cookies when I got back to the albergue just to normalize my sensibilities. When I went to bed that night, I laid on my bunk with my feet in the sleeping bag and the rest of it over me without zipping it up. The bread and cookies had made me so puffy that I couldn't zip my sleeping bag up!

The next morning, I got my things together and went down to the kitchen and made myself an omelet with zucchini, onion, tomato and eggs. I nuked my potato and wrapped it in my bandana for later. I grabbed my pack and walked out of the albergue. I found the arrows and followed them into the wilderness outside of town. The morning was fresh and damp. I walked by a rock wall that was covered with moss of green, pink, and red. It was lovely. The ferns behind it were the edge of a large field with horse stalls in the distance. Everything was so beautiful. I walked and walked past fields of green and fields of brown and up trails and down roads. I came to the Km 50,521 marker with its shell and yellow arrow. I got a café at a bar and an agua grande at the next one. My heart was woozy with love as I advanced past many beautiful scenes of Mother Nature's bounty in Galicia Spain: winding trails edged by zig-zag wooden fences and trees towering toward each other above, little streams seeking their way through the pebbles along the trail, overgrown fields and hills with far off houses, white and grey clouds billowed across the blue sky above a forest of conifers. I walked by a fence that had black and white cows all conglomerating in a corner like they were waiting for someone. Every ear was decorated with a number tag. I saw a bush with flowers that looked like daffodils. The fern fields were accentuated with purple foxglove. There were some beautiful white horses in a field. My book warned me that Burres would be hard to find. The signs were small. I examined all of the signs I could see. I found the turnoff. I walked what seemed to be miles to find my albergue. It was way off of the Camino in a farming community. I started to wish I hadn't selected this albergue. I asked someone in a car and they said to keep walking. When I got there, I went into the bar and got a café Americano. The proprietor told me that I could sign in when his wife arrived. I waited in the bar for her. More people showed up. A woman who was very feminine and beautiful waited with me. She seemed to enjoy everything. Maybe she was as charmed as I was with this beautiful place. Two ladies, a mother and daughter, arrived, saying they had to get a cab from the next town because they missed the sign and walked 2 miles too far. I was glad my angels were working overtime and helped me find the turnoff. When the wife arrived, I signed in, got my bunk, and made reservations for dinner in the dining room.

The next day, the proprietor gave us all a ride back to the Camino. That was nice. The ladies who came in a cab took a cab to the next town. They didn't want to walk that part of the trail a second time. I was on my way to Arca. I called the albergue in Arca and reserved my bed. Glad that he spoke English, I told the man that I would probably not get there till 4 pm and that I needed a lower bunk. He said that was a lot to ask. I told him that I was 70 years old. He said he would see what he could do.

The trail continued through the beautiful wooded farm country. I walked over a freeway on a bright royal-blue-railed bridge into more farm country. Many plastic-coated giant hay bales waited for winter alongside the fields. Fern and dense tree forests, wide meadows and farmlands were spectacular sights. A moss-covered wall had a yellow arrow painted right across the moss. I came to the Km 30,612 marker. It had the colorful graffiti of a red heart and blue star and a poem written in French in black. I got a café Americano in a bar with an interesting whimsical and artsy ceramic statue of a woman on the counter I smiled when I realized there was a beer spigot on the other side. She had a Knights Templar cross on a string around her neck.

I took the trail into the forest again and then down below a freeway under-tunnel guided by signs along the way. In Arca, the albergue as quite large. There were groups and families. The young man was successful in saving a lower bunk for me. I was thankful. The Church in town had a pilgrim's Mass that evening. Afterward, I got a pilgrim's dinner at a nearby restaurant: fish with rice zucchini and some pudding. The waitress brought me a bottle of wine. I told her I just wanted a glass of wine. She told me to drink as much as I wanted and I could leave the rest. Back at the albergue, I went to bed early to beat the snorers.

CHAPTER 22

LAVACOLLA

770 KM

The next morning, I was out early but most left be-fore me. It was crazy in the bathroom with moth-ers organizing their children and people trying to get out of there before 8 am. The bathrooms weren't co-ed, thankfully. I had plenty of time because I went to Mass the night before and had been planning to go in the morning. The cleaning crew came in at 8 am but they didn't bother me.

Walking on my second to the last day, my experience was intensified by the realization that this was it, my last full day of being on this holy transformative journey. It was my last full day to be surrounded by the Camino's beauty. Tomorrow I would walk into Santiago and my mission would be accomplished. As I walked out into the town of Arca, the lady at the door pointed me in the right direction, down the hill and across the street to a trail and a canyon. I walked with the other pilgrims, many of whom had stayed elsewhere the night before, and had been walking already for an hour or more. I came up out of the canyon and into a town. I walked up into a parking lot next to an arena. They were having a gymnastics competition! An MC was shouting words that made the whole arena erupt into boisterous cheering. Excited people were coming and going from the door. I walked on through the parking lot and past a school that had a beautiful 50-foot-long mural of colorful sea creatures and a woman with blue wafting hair. The blue sky was dappled with small clouds. I stopped at a bar for a café Americano, then sauntered through the town and down into another wilderness. I was surrounded on a wide dirt trail by beautiful cedar trees up the slope and down. The sun shone dimly on the trail between the trees. The trail evened out, meandering through a meadow and then through trees again. I think it was a wood lot because it was planted in a big square.

I met with a group of people pushing two men in wheelchairs, one an older man and one a young man. A camera crew was with them. Everyone was smiling and excited to be doing their special Camino. You could tell they revered their wheelchair-bound loved ones. They took turns pushing the wheelchairs. I traveled with them for a while. We both took pictures at a Santiago sculpture along the way. They were going at my speed. I left them when I went into a bar. I was still not feeling one hundred percent in the restroom department. I found a lovely little church that was open. It had a turquoise-colored wooden ceiling and a statue of a kneeling man, hands raised in prayer. A statue of a noble man holding a giant feather was over the altar. A side altar had a beautiful and touching statue of Mary holding the baby Jesus and gazing up into heaven. In contrast, a large picture of a bunch of naked people with fire flaming up onto them hung in a side aisle. They did not look happy.

On the road again, a high wooden sign shaped like an upside-down L had a shell, an arrow and the words "Camino de Santiago." It was surrounded by foliage and purple fox glove. The formerly yellow flowered bushes were all covered with their silvery pods. I walked out of the wilderness into the town of Lavacolla, which my book told me, means "wash your private parts." The early pilgrims stopped there and washed themselves before they went into Santiago. Seems the people in the 1200s didn't wash, and the priests in Santiago complained of the stench of the pilgrims. I was the first one to arrive at the albergue, which hadn't opened yet. I decided to walk around the town to find the church and a mercado. I asked a man on the street where the Iglesia was. He pointed up a road and made a curving motion. I walked and found the church. The town was lovely with many well-tended flowering gardens. Mass was at noon. I got there just in time. The small church was stately with a high, white, curved ceiling and angels by a cloudy view into heaven were above the portico above the altar. Interestingly the statue of a noble man with a large white feather was above the altar and the picture of naked people with fire coming up on them was on the wall. I loved being there for Mass.

After Mass, I noticed a restaurant at the bottom of the hill near the church. I saw that there was a bowl of beans on most of the tables. I sat down on the patio and asked for a bowl of beans. The waitress didn't understand me and walked away. It turned out that the beans were complimentary with the beer, so I had to order beer to get the beans. They were really delicious with a thick broth from the pig's knuckles in them.

I went back to the albergue to wait with a few more people for it to open. A table and bench were on the porch, so I sat there. A woman came out and sat at another table and started checking pilgrims in. I got my lower bunk near the bathroom in the dimly lit bunk house. Checking out the kitchen in the building out back, I found dishes but no pots. It had a microwave and a coffee pot as well. The laundry was in a room next door and a massive area of clothes lines was out back. I got my dirty clothes and gave some euros to the guy who put them in the washer. He said to come back in 30 minutes.

The lady at the desk inside told me where the mercado was. I rested while I waited for my clothes. I ran out of soap right before I got to Lavacolla, so it was fitting that I got a new bar at the store there. They only had a two-bar pack of the soap I liked, so I donated the other one to the pilgrim's closet at the albergue. Since the albergue didn't have a complete kitchen, I just purchased my vegetables and sausage and some corn nuts for my last day on the road. I got my clothes off the line when I returned.

At dinner time, the lady at the desk pointed down the road and said I'd find a restaurant down there. I walked and found that the restaurant was the same as the one down the hill from the church. I walked in and told the bartender I wanted the pilgrim's dinner. He said to wait there. A waitress came and ushered me into the back dining room. There were a few people eating in the dining room family style at long tables. I got the chicken, rice, and veggies with some creamy yogurt dessert. They brought me a bottle of wine. The food was basic and filling. A boisterous group came in: a laughing wife, her amused husband, and another couple. They had a lot of fun making jokes about each other's names.

I went to bed right away when I got back. I wanted to get up early and enjoy my walk into Santiago. Across the street from the albergue was another of the wooden upside down L signs announcing the trail to Santiago with a shell and yellow arrow. It led to a black top road, down into the wilderness. The topography was a bit drier, although it was green. I saw an horreo outside of a farm house. A wooden walkway took me down and over a fast-moving stream with cottonwood trees on each bank. The morning was misty and a bit foggy. I couldn't see far ahead. Birds were singing. I walked up a hill with ferns on each side. When I started the Camino, the ferns were just popping up; now they were tall. Vines covered the trees. Everything was blissfully beautiful. I came to a town and got a coffee at a bar. I passed a manhole cover that had a shell motif in the center. A giant sculpture with a glass cross that had a shell at the center and two pilgrims standing was up on a grassy hill beside the road. I went into a simple little church with just six pews to stop and rest and pray. In the chaplet was a statue of Mary Queen of Heaven on one side, St. Joseph on the other, and a Pieta (Mary holding her dead son Jesus on her lap) over the altar. Walking on, I went up over a hill and got my first glimpse of the city of Santiago in the misty distance. Each side of the road became grassy like a park. A handsome statue of "El Templario Peregrino" was on one side, and further on was a large bronze statue of a dancing starfish. A triumphal arch clad with statues of saints stood at the side of the road. A low Santiago de Compostela sign was decorated by enthusiastic pilgrims with stickers and tied bandanas, flags and ribbons. I walked under a pergola path covered with wisteria. Next to it I got a bird's eye view of a neighborhood of modern tract homes. New and ancient business buildings stood next to each other along the road. And then the dirt trail took off into a park. In the town of Santiago, it was hard to tell which way to go because I didn't see many arrows. A man yelled to me and, pointing, he told me to go up another road. He was a pilgrim who was tethered to another disabled pilgrim. He was looking out for his charge and me too! He steered me in the right direction a couple of times. He even took me in a public elevator up to a higher street. After that, I followed them for a while. I saw the Santiago cathedral above the buildings and tried to figure out how to get there. The streets were winding and went into each other so it was hard to tell which way to go. I heard the bagpipe and knew I was close. A man stood on the wide path that led to the cathedral. He played his bag pipe which echoed loudly between the buildings while people walked by him. He had his case opened for donations. A woman was on her knees, hands clasped, and praying. A bowl with some coins in it was laid on the ground in-front of her. I was so mesmerized that I walked right past them without thinking to reach for my coin purse. I finally got to the cathedral. The square in front of it was full of people. Some were just arriving and some looked like they were laying out sunning themselves, basking in the cathedral's glory. I found a woman and asked her to take my picture. I raised my hands in victory and smiled. 780 km or 484.67 miles complete.

AFTERWARD

After I got my picture in front of the cathedral, I went to find the pilgrim's office to get my official Compostela certificate. I stood in line for an hour and a half as it wound around the building, through the garden and down hall ways. I heard the line was usually longer. My time in line was spent talking about American politics and many things with a father and daughter from Norway. When it was my turn, I showed my passport and my certificate with all my colorful stamps. The clerk told me I was supposed to get it stamped twice a day during the last 100 k. I told her I heard I only needed to do that if I hadn't walked the whole way. She studied my certificate to make sure I was really there the whole time. The clerk consulted with another official. Finally, they decided to give me my Compostela certificate. Phew.

I found the hotel where I had a reservation. An ice cream concession was in front of it. The lady stepped away from the ice cream counter and took my name and credit card information. She said I could come back later to get my pack, which was locked up until the hotel proprietor returned. My room, on the third floor, was modern, quiet, and comfortable.

It's a tradition to get a haircut after completing the Camino. I found a styling salon. The stylist was leery of cutting my hair because he didn't speak English and he was afraid he wouldn't understand what I wanted. I motioned to cut it short. I got my hair cut short in Paris before I started the Camino so I would be able to control my hair with a little comb, one of the ways I kept my pack as light as possible. I wanted it short again. The stylist was an artist. He gave me an excellent precision cut. I saw a spa and looked up in my translator how to ask to get my eyebrows waxed.

I was starting to feel human again. I saw a dress shop and went in and bought a dress or two that would go with my shower shoes. None of the stores had attractive shoes that fit me.

When I got back to the hotel, I found that Mass had been earlier, so I would have to go to Mass the next day. I got a good night's sleep in my very comfortable bed. The next day, I extended my stay and was given a small room on the ground floor. I could hear the street noise.

It was the year before the Holy Year. The cathedral was closed for repairs and not having the traditional pilgrim Mass. They were, however, letting pilgrims in to kiss the statue. The next day, I went to the cathedral, kissed the large golden statue of St. James, and laid a red rose at the crypt. I went to mass at one of the auxiliary churches that were open for pilgrims.

I spent the day near the cathedral and joyfully watched many pilgrims come into the square completing their journey. I made a reservation to take a bus tour to Finisterre and Muxia in the morning. I bought a few mementos to bring home with me. I still had only my backpack and bag to carry all my possessions.

The bus trip to Finisterre and Muxia was spectacular. Our driver was personable, informative, and entertaining. He explained to us that we had all been bitten by the Camino bug and we would return to walk again and again. He took us to historic sites and told us stories that made me love the place. We had lunch in Finisterre at a seafood restaurant. I had a dish I remember Shirley from Holland sent me a picture of on our WhatsApp. It had many sizes and shapes of clams in their open shells arranged on a bed of shredded lettuce. Seeing the ocean at Finisterre was wonderful. I found it pleasurable to sit and gaze over rippling blue water below a heavenly blue sky.

I'm looking forward to returning to the Camino and walk in Portugal next time. The Camino Portuguese is shorter. I won't be so worn out and will hopefully be able to walk to Finisterre and Muxia afterwards. I would also love to walk, another time, along the northern coast of Spain on the Camino del Norte, maybe with one of my kids or grandchildren.

The changes I plan to make to keep myself healthy and happy when I come back to the Camino are as follows: keep myself hydrated by drinking two agua grandes each day. I'm going to bring lightweight containers for my lunch so I won't have to put it on bread. I will use my good ear plugs to get sleep, and stay more often in a hotel if I find it hard to sleep in the Albergues. I'll pare down my possessions to have a lighter pack. I've already purchased a down sleeping bag that weighs much less. I'll bring three skirts with tights and no long pants. I'm going to study reviews of waterproof hiking boots to find ones that actually are waterproof. I plan to praise God and keep a good thought so my vibration will be high and I'll be attracting good experiences. In the meantime, I'll keep reminding myself that all of life is a Camino and all time is sacred.

ACKNOWLEDGEMENTS

I extend special gratitude to my sister-in-law, Bernadette Donnelly, who took it upon herself to prepare me for walking up mountains on the Camino by taking me on hikes up mountains near home. To my friend Syvera Hardy I express thanks for walking 5 miles with me twice a week for years which helped me know I could walk 5 miles before lunch and 5 miles after lunch. I recognize Zia who taught me Tai Chi walking. I am particularly pleased to thank the Magic Horse Therapeutic Riding Center for preparing me to walk by helping me develop a strong core from toting wheel barrows of horse leavings. I gratefully acknowledge Jack Miller and the Phoenix Project for introducing me to sacred time and encouraged me to accomplish my dreams. To Judy Meeker who planted the seed that started me wanting to walk the Camino, thank you. I owe a debt of gratitude to my Facebook friends who prayed for me and made me feel like I wasn't alone by commenting on my posts from the Camino. It is with a great fondness that I acknowledge my adult children and their spouses: Lisa and Dan, Peter and Renae, Carla, Cecilia and Topher, John and Monica who were my sounding boards for my more-gory details on the WhatsApp that Carla set up for me entitled "Mom's Walkabout Check-in." I am beholden to my "comadre" Mary Gomez and her daughter, Linda Fierro who let me read my book to them They helped me by making suggestions where the words were just not right. I tender thanks to my sister, Maureen Rymer who did the first and second edits on my book and to my editor, Wayne Purdin, and Meg Goldfeather, Lani Stacks, and Richard Sturgill who edited too. It is because of Ellaine Ursuy who guided me through the book writing process and everyone at Self-Publishing School who taught me so much along the way, that this book exists. A heartfelt thank you to everyone on the launch team for reading and reviewing.

ABOUT THE AUTHOR

Kathleen Donnelly Israel was born 1949 in San Diego, CA where she has lived her whole life. She is a devout Catholic. Ron and Kathleen Israel raised their five children in Lakeside, San Diego county. They were a Team Couple for Worldwide Marriage Encounter in the 70s and 80s.

She has a Bachelor's Degree in Art from San Diego State University. She studied Expressive Arts Therapy at the European Graduate School in Switzerland. She is a certified Transformational Breathing Facilitator, Theta Healer, and has enjoyed a lifetime of walking, hiking, and running.

Kathleen cared for her husband for the 17 years that he had Parkinson's disease till he died in 2018. During this time, she studied spiritual healing from many enlightened thought leaders and teachers. This is her first book.

Self-Publishing
School

NOW IT'S YOUR TURN

Discover the EXACT 3-step blueprint you need to become a bestselling author in as little as 3 months.

Self-Publishing School helped me, and now I want them to help you with this FREE resource to begin outlining your book!

Even if you're busy, bad at writing, or don't know where to start, you CAN write a bestseller and build your best life.

With tools and experience across a variety of niches and professions, Self-Publishing School is the only resource you need to take your book to the finish line!

DON'T WAIT

Say "YES" to becoming a bestseller:
https://self-publishingschool.com/friend/

Follow the steps on the page to get a FREE resource to get started on your book and unlock a discount to get started with Self-Publishing School

Made in the USA
Las Vegas, NV
22 August 2021